THE WELLNESS ASSET

SONAL UBEROI

www.get-known.co.uk

CONTENTS

This Book is For: 5

This Book is Not For: 7

This Book Will: 9

Meet Sonal   11

How to Use this Book   13

The Hotelier of the Future   17

PART 1   22
THE WELLNESS OPPORTUNITY

CHAPTER 1   25
What's going wrong with wellness in hospitality?

CHAPTER 2   37
Three Fallacies

PART 2   52
MY APPROACH

CHAPTER 3   55
My Story

CHAPTER 4   67
The Harsh Truths of Wellness in Hospitality

PART 3   78
THE ESSENCE MODEL

CHAPTER 5   81
Introduction to the ESSENCE Model

CHAPTER 6   95
Expectation

CHAPTER 7   129
Story

CHAPTER 8   161
System

CHAPTER 9   189
Execution

CHAPTER 10   225
Navigation

CHAPTER 11   257
Consistency

CHAPTER 12   287
Engagement

PART 4   320
WHAT INNOVATIVE AND
FORWARD-THINKING HOTELIERS ARE DOING

CHAPTER 13   323
ESSENCE in Practice

CHAPTER 14   343
Next Steps

Glossary   349

Acknowledgements   351

THIS BOOK IS FOR:

I wrote this book for hoteliers like you, who want to survive the current challenges in the industry and thrive long into the future:

- You have suffered financially during the COVID-19 pandemic and unfortunately have had to let go of staff, many of them loyal, committed and talented

- You understand that the elements you relied on in the past – such as business travel, group bookings and large-scale events (from conferences to weddings) – are gone, and are looking at ways to replace that income

- You recognise that things have changed and that you need to evolve and adapt to the realities of the post-pandemic market, but you are unsure of the best way forward

- You know that waiting for things to go back to the way they were is not a viable strategy

- The wellness offering at your hotel might have historically underperformed or been sublet to a third-party operator which is now struggling to survive, or you might not have a wellness offering in your hotel at all. You've seen wellness offerings do well for others and think they might have potential, but don't want to make a bad investment decision

You see this as an opportunity to break away from the traditional model and come out of this with a stronger, more unique offering, one that guests absolutely love and recommend organically. You want to be part of this industry's vibrant future, not to fade away like one of its dinosaurs.

If you are a hotel general manager, owner, hospitality consultant or professional who considers yourself a hotelier at heart, and you are open to innovation – I wrote this book for you.

THIS BOOK IS <u>NOT</u> FOR:

The traditional hoteliers.

The ones who want to continue to do hospitality the way they have always done it, who want to continue to rely heavily on what has been their main demographic: business travel and conferences.

The ones who hold on to the hope that one day things will eventually return to how they were before the pandemic hit, before they were thrown into a standstill overnight. In the meantime, they are looking for quick fixes and inexpensive Band-Aid solutions to survive a rough period and stay afloat. They still believe in the traditional bricks-and-mortar business model that got them profits in the past.

They're the Blackberry of hospitality.

THIS BOOK WILL:

This book will help you to leverage the untapped asset that holds the most potential right in front of you: wellness.

It will:

- Show you how the market leaders are getting wellness right while most are underperforming

- Inspire you as to what is possible using wellness at your hotel, both right now and in the future

- Dispel the myths that have traditionally surrounded wellness within hospitality

- Give you a proven ESSENCE roadmap to guide you from idea to execution

- Prevent you from wasting time and money on poor wellness decisions and investments.

In this book, I will show you how to transform your business by embracing and adopting wellness as a core part of your brand. With this shift in mindset, you will maximise the exciting opportunities wellness offers for your hotel.

This book will not tell you about the latest trend, the shiniest new equipment, or the latest technology on restorative therapy. Nor is it a magic wand that will miraculously change your hotel.

It will, however, give you a sure-fire way to futureproof your business. It provides the essential tools so that you can build the right (and most profitable) wellness concept for your hotel.

MEET SONAL

Sonal Uberoi is:

- A top international wellness expert and founder of Spa Balance, a boutique consultancy that specialises in wellness concepts for hotels worldwide

- Curator of the Spa Sommelier, a multi-award-winning fusion wellness concept

- Host of the *Wellness in Hospitality* interview series (available in podcast and as LinkedIn articles), in which she talks to thought leaders in hospitality; guests have included Fernando Gibaja, Rocco Bova and John Nielsen

- On a mission to craft a meaningful legacy through making a positive impact in people's lives, a landmark that will be appreciated for generations to come

- A wellness enthusiast. She practises what she preaches and leads a well life in the beautiful, vibrant city of Madrid.

Sonal Uberoi has:

- Combined the best of both worlds, as a wellness expert with a former life as a financial analyst in a top investment bank

- Co-founded a fusion dining concept in London

- Been there, done that and got the T-shirt several times. When it comes to wellness; she knows what works and what doesn't

- Designed a unique and proven model to show hoteliers how to not only survive, but thrive, by putting wellness at the core

- A multicultural background, with work and life experience on four continents.

Sonal often hangs out on LinkedIn where she shares expert insights. You can connect with her at:

https://www.linkedin.com/in/sonaluberoi/

or check out her work at:

https://www.spa-balance.com/

HOW TO USE THIS BOOK

This book is your go-to reference for wellness. It is your business playbook that contains the essential tools for you to do wellness successfully in any hotel you'll work in (even when you leave your current hotel and move to another one).

I want to show you the true power of wellness to transform your hotel. To do that, we need to take an accurate temperature reading of where your business is at right now before we start. Coming from a finance background, I'm a firm believer in having measures and metrics. I'll ask you to do this again when we get to the end of the book so you can see in black and white just how much progress you've made (and share this with any stakeholders you need to get on board).

So before we start, head over to **www.spa-balance.com/essence-scorecard/** and take my ESSENCE scorecard. You don't need to do any preparation – it's just a simple series of questions that I've carefully designed to give you the most meaningful 'snapshot' of where you are and where your potential opportunities lie. Answer the questions honestly to get an accurate benchmark. You'll get a report highlighting the key strengths and weaknesses around your wellness offering today and what areas you can improve on as you read along. It's a great (and free!) tool to learn more about your capability to create a wellness asset at this present moment.

In Part 1, we'll reframe your current view of wellness and show you some common fallacies. In Part 2, we'll learn the harsh truths of wellness in hospitality and how you can work around them. Then grab a pen and notepad for Part 3, because this is where the heavy lifting begins. I'll walk you through my proven ESSENCE model and guide you through the exercises I do with clients to help them build a profitable wellness asset. I know you're busy, so to make things easier for you I've created my Wellness Business Essentials Toolkit which contains all the worksheets and templates you'll need to work through each of the stages.

This comprehensive toolkit will:

- Save you time and energy focusing on the small stuff, like how to collate the information in a coherent and easy-to-access way, so that instead you can focus on the big-picture stuff – the content.

- Allow you to easily share important information with your teams in a concise and accessible way, instead of preparing long reports that don't provide much benefit.

- Give you a set of working documents that you (and your team) can go back to and update as you're working on your business.

- Serve as a priceless resource you can take with you to your next hotel.

You can download my Wellness Business Essentials Toolkit here:
www.spa-balance.com/wellness-business-essentials-toolkit/.

Don't just read it once and then go on with business as usual. Keep it handy and refer to it often. Keep a pencil, notebook and highlighter close so that you can make notes and highlight sections as you read along. Also, don't keep it to yourself. Give a copy of the book to each of your department heads (for example, your directors of rooms, sales and marketing, food and beverage, and wellness), because the business principles I share in this book don't only apply to wellness; they can be extrapolated to other areas of the hotel.

THE HOTELIER OF THE FUTURE

In the course of researching this book, I have met some truly inspirational hoteliers– passionate men and women who are leading the way, seeing wellness as a core part of hospitality.

These hoteliers of the future are pivoting, adapting and thriving by building and leveraging their wellness asset to enhance their guests' overall experience in their hotel.

They understand that their guests' needs have evolved and that today's business and leisure travellers want more than the standard hotel room, decent breakfast and beautiful facilities. Today's guests want experiences that are fulfilling, memorable and shareable; they want experiences that transform their overall wellbeing, even if it's in a simple way.

And these passionate men and women know the only way they can transform their guests' wellbeing is through focusing on the wellbeing of their teams and surrounding community. They attract people who think alike, and they get their teams excited about their vision and the positive impact of their meaningful work. They create a growth environment with wellness at its core.

The hotelier of the future is forward-thinking, audacious and legacy-oriented, with a vision that stretches far beyond short-term profitability.

FORWARD-THINKING

These passionate men and women who are leading the way understand that the hospitality industry is a solid, established industry with people at the core of its philosophy. However, they also realise they need to go that extra mile to regain the kind of market appraisal and consumer confidence in hospitality that goes beyond safe and clean facilities.

They have carefully observed the shifting market conditions since the 2020 pandemic and have embraced the wellness renaissance that is reinvigorating the market. They are not making knee-jerk decisions and slashing costs to the detriment of their guests' and team's experience. They have understood that if they do not catch this tide and pivot their businesses, their hotels will eventually become obsolete as the new generation of wellness-minded entrepreneurs gains market share.

These visionary hoteliers leverage the people aspect of their business; they revive the true spirit of hospitality and make the human-ness of the industry their central focus. They know that the secret ingredient in the mix is their people. Their teams – the people who wake up each morning and come to work thinking about how they can make their guests' experience truly special – are their superpower, and they are something other industries trying to jump on the wellness bandwagon don't have.

AUDACIOUS

These passionate men and women who are championing wellness in hospitality are bold and courageous and willing to challenge the way things have traditionally been done.

"

THEY SEE THEIR BUSINESS
THROUGH THE REAL LENS OF
THEIR TRUE POTENTIAL

"

They are willing to try new things and they actively explore all the avenues available to them, all the while keeping their ear to the ground, listening to their guests and thoughtfully implementing new offerings.

They are open-minded and question their current business model and their products and services ecosystem. They understand the critical nature of the situation and are acutely aware of how important it is for their owners and shareholders to see a return on investment. They are brave when fighting for the needs of their teams and securing the right talent to develop those teams so they can pave the way forward for the new, reinvigorated hospitality industry.

They take calculated risks to push their hospitality business up a notch. They use wellness strategically, as a tool to achieve their overall goal of enhancing the wellbeing of their guests. They break away from the limited definition of what wellness has meant in the hospitality industry and seamlessly integrate it into their asset ecosystem.

LEGACY OVER PROFITABILITY

These passionate men and women who are shaping the future of hospitality care deeply about their industry. While they recognise the importance of delivering on budgetary expectations, for them success goes beyond profitability. Increasing profits by 20% means little when that objective has been reached through the age-old measures of cost-cutting – reducing headcount and streamlining costs.

These visionary leaders do not look for quick fixes or Band-Aid solutions. They invest time and money into futureproofing their businesses. This means they design their offering so it continues to be relevant and deliver value well into the future, constantly evolving and responding to changing market conditions. They know that a strong and robust system takes time to implement and requires the right expertise.

They are in it for the long run. They want to leave behind a legacy that will have a positive impact on the hospitality industry. They want their footprint to be sensed through every hotel they manage and their business to be a landmark of innovation, adaptability and guest experiences.

These visionary hoteliers are part of the new breed of entrepreneurs who care about the social and environmental impact their decisions as key business leaders have on the overall wellbeing of the destination they operate within. They see their business through the real lens of their true potential: the potential to be landmarks.

After living through the extreme market conditions and measures of the 2020 pandemic, the hoteliers of the future realise they actually don't need to look very far for the way forward. The solution to all their problems has been staring them in the face: it lies in wellness. This book is going to show you how you can be one of these hoteliers of the future.

You can read the insights shared by these passionate men and women in my *Wellness in Hospitality* interview series on LinkedIn: **www.linkedin.com/in/sonaluberoi/.**

PART 1
THE WELLNESS OPPOR-TUNITY

'IN EVERY SITUATION, WE STILL HAVE TWO WAYS OF LOOKING AT IT. WE CAN EITHER TAKE IT AS AN OPPORTUNITY AND LOOK AT THE POSITIVE SIDE OF IT AND SEE HOW QUICKLY WE CAN RESPOND PROACTIVELY... OR WE WAIT FOR THE WHOLE THING TO TAKE OVER AND TAKE THE BEATING.'

- YAGNA PRATHAP

CHAPTER 1
WHAT'S GOING WRONG WITH WELLNESS IN HOSPITALITY?

WHAT IS WELLNESS?

Wellness is the new buzzword. Nearly all businesses across all industries worldwide are embracing the idea in some way, shape or form, either to redefine their processes or philosophy or to enhance their product and service offering. But what does wellness actually mean?

There are many competing definitions in circulation. For example, the Global Wellness Institute defines wellness as 'the active pursuit of activities, choices and lifestyles that lead to a state of holistic health', while the National Wellness Institute defines wellness as 'a conscious, self-directed and evolving process of achieving full potential.'

As you can see, these are quite broad and generic definitions that refer to an individual's pursuit of essentially a better state of being or health; they don't specify what products and services constitute wellness, and this gives each industry, business and profession the flexibility to adapt wellness in its own unique way.

So what does wellness actually mean in the hospitality industry? Wellness is more than a signature massage, a spa, a showpiece gym, or a sunset yoga session. Its effects reach beyond the physical realm of the hotel's facilities and offerings and are felt more deeply.

When wellness works in a hotel, it works because it has been treated holistically and forms an integral part of the guest experience; it touches all aspects of the business, from every corner of the property, the offering, the people and the concept to the values, culture and mindset of the hoteliers. It is made up of many small but significant moments which, when meaningfully thought through, influence how our guests sleep, the experience of what they eat, how they interact with their surroundings, how they feel when they are in our hotels and how our staff engage with them. It impacts our guests before they arrive at our properties and continues to affect them long after they have left.

Wellness encompasses the essence of our business, of everything that makes us what we are. It is part of the DNA of our brand.

WELLNESS VERSUS WELLBEING

We see 'wellness' and 'wellbeing' mistakenly being used interchangeably. However, there is a subtle yet important difference we must get right. Although closely related, these terms are not synonymous.

A simple way to view it is as follows: wellness is the tool and wellbeing the goal.

Wellness provides us with the tools that allow us to access different types of wellbeing (e.g., physical, mental, emotional, spiritual) – our goals. These wellness tools include touch therapies, alternative medicine, fitness activities, a balanced diet and a gamut of other services designed to enhance our mental, physical, emotional and spiritual wellbeing.

Hotels that confuse these terms end up with very short-term strategies. They mistakenly design or pivot their wellness offerings around the tools (e.g., the latest technology in restorative therapy or shiny new touchless equipment) instead of the goal (e.g., enhanced mental wellbeing).

Of course, we too can provide the latest technology in restorative therapy or the shiny new touchless equipment (the tools), but we will not help our guests achieve their overall wellbeing goal – that feeling of being 'well' – if they drink five cups of coffee a day, lead a sedentary life or suffer from family disharmony due to a high-pressure job. The moment they stumble upon their first obstacle to improving their wellbeing – which they inevitably will, as the journey to wellbeing is rarely smooth – they'll be drawn to a newer and flashier piece of equipment or therapy that promises them the results they want. In which case, our entire offering and wellness concept will no longer appeal to them.

I am not saying we should not specialise or go niche with our wellness offering. What I am saying is that you must not mistake the tool or the means to achieve a certain goal for the goal itself. When we design our wellness concept based on a tool instead of a goal, we run the danger of having unsuccessful or obsolete offerings and facilities.

A GAME-CHANGER FOR THE GUEST

Have you ever walked into a hotel, a restaurant, a shop, a spa or any other public space and felt a great sense of contentment, where everything seemed just perfect? Perhaps you couldn't believe that this feeling would continue beyond the first magical moments of your arrival, but it did. You couldn't pinpoint what exactly it was that made you feel so wonderful and at ease, as the delightful whole was a sum of many small pleasures – the interactions with the staff, the customer journey, the design of the space, the lighting, the smell, the temperature and so on. These all combined to create a unique and memorable experience. This essentially is how it feels for your guests when wellness (the tool) has been threaded thoughtfully and meaningfully throughout their hotel experience to keep their overall wellbeing (the goal) in mind.

It is that first moment they book your hotel, that first interaction with your staff, that excitement building up as their holiday approaches. It is their favourite dish, the heavenly treatment, the beautiful space in a quiet corner where they can read or the fitness kit that allows them to work out in the comfort of their room when they want to. It is your therapist

"

WELLNESS IS A GREAT
OPPORTUNITY FOR BUSINESSES TO
EXPONENTIALLY INCREASE THEIR
REVENUE

"

thoughtfully checking in on them after their stay; that nudge to help them get back on their wellness regime when the reality of the daily grind makes it all too easy to get off track. This is the power of wellness.

Wellness has become the new luxury that today's consumers are looking to our industry to provide as they pursue that state of wellbeing that allows for a fuller human experience than traditional hospitality typically provides. It has become standard to find a spa and gym in five-star luxury hotels, but the market now demands increasingly more sophisticated, integrated wellness experiences.

Guests now crave a sense of connection from a hotel stay. Whatever the reason for their trip, people who are travelling less want to travel better; they want to be nourished, healed, surprised and delighted, from before they arrive to during their stay and beyond.

This is exactly what having an integrated wellness offering can do for your guests.

A GAME-CHANGER FOR THE INVESTORS

Investors want to be reassured that wherever they put their money, they will get a coherent return on investment. Wellness is a great opportunity for businesses to exponentially increase their revenue, and in turn, their return on investment.

We're already seeing how companies in other industries like ours, with the same deeply ingrained traditional mindset, are successfully using wellness to transform their businesses and carve a niche in today's environment. Let's take the example of Greggs, the UK's largest bakery chain, and the soar-away success of its vegan sausage roll. Greggs, a regular mass-market bakery, recognised the increasing number of vegans in the UK (a 360% increase over the past 10 years, the fastest growing lifestyle shift in the UK), and took its time (three years) to create a product to attract this discerning, environmentally aware and wellbeing-conscious customer, without losing the essence of the company brand.

Greggs' vegan sausage roll sat so well alongside its more traditional products that non-vegans wanted to try it. The company's turnover and profits soared, contributing to a year-on-year sales increase of 13.5%. Its success was due to careful planning, sensible timing (January 2019, the sixth 'Veganuary' in which a record 40,000 people pledged to try a vegan diet for a month), and a company-wide strategy that recognised the true potential of this wellness-conscious movement. Greggs, essentially a traditional 80-year-old fast-food institution, is a perfect example of how to make the most of the untapped potential of wellness to completely pivot your offering and reinvent a brand, while staying true to your brand's essence. You can download the full Greggs case study here **www.spa-balance.com/resources/greggs-case-study/.**

Traditionally, hoteliers have opted for the asset-light approach of owning fewer assets and maximising profits. This approach worked well for the larger hotel chains that wanted to curb risk and deliver their owners swift returns on investment – but it only worked during the economic boom and relatively small economic downturns. When the pandemic of 2020 prevented predominantly service-oriented, bricks-and-mortar operations from opening their doors, hoteliers realised they didn't have a solid asset ecosystem to fall back on as they had built their businesses around optimising profits per square metre and, as a result, had become over-reliant on one demographic: business travel and conferences. This approach was doomed to fail; in Chapter 2, I'll explain why.

Wellness, when carefully threaded through a hotel's asset ecosystem, makes the entire ecosystem more robust. It allows investors to create businesses that don't rely solely on one source of income, but instead generate income from diverse and non-traditional sources – they maximise areas other than rooms. Greggs is a perfect example.

A GAME-CHANGER FOR THE STAFF

Wellness does not only enhance our guests' experience; it also enhances our staff's experience during their tenure with us and beyond.

Since the start of 2020, many hoteliers have had the distasteful job of laying off loyal, talented and dedicated team members and of reducing the salaries of those few who remain, to survive the impact of the pandemic. From the employee's side, many have discovered that hospitality is no longer the 'safe' industry in which they knew they could get a job and grow within a specific brand. They have also discovered that their salaries are no longer secure. Those who were lucky enough to keep their jobs found themselves working more and taking on additional responsibility – and, in some cases, for a substantially lower wage.

The consequences of these actions will be felt over the years to come. There is the danger that we will permanently lose this great talent to other industries, and perhaps find it more challenging to hire it back as our offering might be less appealing from a salary, brand promise and work–life balance perspective.

We know that hospitality is not a career path for the faint-hearted. Long, antisocial hours (themselves an impediment to wellness) and demanding guests are the norm in our industry. That said, there is also no other industry out there that allows you to travel to and live in beautiful destinations and interact with people from all over the world. People who choose to work in hospitality choose it for all these unparalleled perks that other sectors simply can't match.

Wellness makes the work environment of your teams rewarding in a holistic sense and helps you to attract and retain sought-after talent on your teams. With wellness, you put the wellbeing of your staff front and centre, alongside that of your guests. It allows you to provide your teams with the right tools to enhance their wellbeing and encourage a healthy work–life balance.

Wellness can position hospitality as the most desirable industry for wellbeing professionals to work in: an innovative industry that has a meaningful impact not only on the staff but also on the local community.

AN OPPORTUNITY FOR A LANDMARK LEGACY

I have very vivid and fond memories of grabbing every chance I could to tag along with my father during his site visits back home in Kenya. He was a structural and civil engineer who, apart from designing and building key structures like dams, bridges and highways, also designed and built hotels. I distinctly remember one of his projects in Nairobi, where the owner insisted on having the swimming pool jutting out of the side of the building, with no visible supporting beams under or over the structure, so it appeared the pool was 'hanging' over the driveway to the entrance – something the entire design team declared technically impossible and discarded outright. This was nearly 40 years ago, when it was unthinkable for hotel design teams to dare to challenge the norm in any part of the world, let alone in Africa.

My father was expected to accept the status quo and to follow the traditional way of designing yet another rooftop bling-bling pool. A sucker for challenges, with a track record of breaking away from outdated norms, my father boldly announced that he would make the owner's wish possible. Now, which owner could say no to that?

So, my father set himself and his team of draftsmen to work, day and night, for what seemed like forever. The design team and international consultants, who were at first sceptical about the possibility of designing such a pool and then reticent about sharing their excitement about doing something so different, saw my father making progress on his mission impossible and gradually started dropping by his office at all hours of the day, enthusiastically putting forward suggestions and ideas to make that 'hanging' swimming pool possible.

Lo and behold, my father and his team delivered on the owner's wish – the owner had his hanging swimming pool, the first of its type in East Africa. It still stands today, nearly four decades later.

In the world of hotels, that project was the landmark legacy of each and every person involved in it. My father, along with all the people who wanted to do something that was not just different but truly excellent, saw the opportunity to pivot the design of hotels. They dared to go against the rigid standards laid down by international hotel chains, not to gratuitously challenge the status quo, but to better the way things were done. They wanted to do amazing things that could be seen and appreciated for generations to come. They wanted to leave a meaningful legacy behind – one that truly changed the way things were done in their line of work.

We're living in truly unique times and we have the opportunity to make a real difference in our industry. We, too, have the power to leave a meaningful legacy behind and change the rules of the game.

CHAPTER 2
THREE
FALLACIES

Traditional hoteliers know that wellness is something they need to offer, but they haven't quite figured out the right formula to tap into its full potential. They struggle to define their wellness offering in a way that helps them stand out from the competition and also makes them money without a sizeable capital outlay and no return on investment.

The main areas traditional hoteliers struggle with when it comes to wellness are:

- **Concept:** They lack a clearly defined wellness concept; there is often little to no difference between one hotel's wellness offering and the other's next door. Their wellness facilities have grown organically over time and have been squeezed into any available space to maximise revenue per square metre.

- **People:** They lack the right expertise and people to do wellness properly in their hotels. They struggle to find qualified and experienced talent that their wellness profit and loss can sustain. They promote under-qualified staff to oversee their wellness operations, and as a result, these operations become a constant source of headache.

- **Performance:** They ambitiously invest large sums in building grand facilities – large hydrothermal areas, fully equipped spa suites, beautiful treatment rooms, state-of-the-art gyms – only to find later that they have a heavily subsidised operation with high overheads and no return on investment.

They struggle with these areas because they've fallen victim to one or more of the three common fallacies around wellness in hospitality: false perceptions, false economies and false profits. Each of these fallacies, along with its own set of associated myths, is the result of a traditional mindset that has led hoteliers down unhelpful paths.

FALSE PERCEPTIONS

A common fallacy around wellness in hospitality is false perceptions. This fallacy leads traditional hoteliers to mistakenly believe that wellness is not a lucrative option for them to fully explore. As a result, they either under-invest in their wellness offering, treat it as an amenity to their core business, or stick to what they know best: selling rooms and food and beverage.

Myth 1: 'It's only 1–3% of revenue.'

The traditionalist's mindset

The traditionalists believe that as wellness is only a small part of their overall business, it doesn't make sense for them to concentrate on it. As a result, they under-invest in their wellness offering, dedicating little time, attention or resources to it. They still focus on external and very visible trappings to impress guests – for example, a grand lobby – rather than on giving guests a holistic experience. With this mindset, they attract a less loyal customer who is looking for the next good deal instead of a unique experience – a customer who is not willing to spend more. Traditionalists' wellness offerings continue to underperform, the traditionalists continue to underinvest, and the vicious cycle continues.

Myth buster: 'It's what will keep us in business.'

The innovator's mindset

The innovators see wellness as their opportunity to pivot and respond to changing market conditions. They understand that wellness generates not only direct revenue, but also substantial indirect revenue through higher occupancy, average rates, average spend and length of stay. They tap into a more discerning client who looks for quality wellness experiences, spends more in their restaurants, stays longer, and repeats if the experience is right. Innovators outperform their competitors because they look beyond the direct revenues of their wellness offering, just like Greggs looked beyond its vegan sausage roll, and explore the full potential of what responding to this global wellness-conscious movement can do for their overall business.

Myth 2: 'It's just another amenity.'

The traditionalist's mindset

The traditionalists believe their main business is selling room nights and food and beverages. They classify their wellness offering as an amenity department that supports their core business. Their business strategy focuses on using their wellness offering to sell more room nights– for example, a special Valentine's offer of a free couple's massage with a weekend stay. As a result, they rarely have wellness offerings that stand out from those of their competitors and their guests receive the same cookie-cutter hospitality experience in every hotel of the same category. Traditionalists' wellness offerings continue to be ordinary, minor operating departments instead of strong revenue generators.

Myth buster: 'It's why our guests come to us.'

The innovator's mindset

The innovators know their guests don't come to their hotel because of its rooms or fancy bars; their guests choose this hotel because they want to live remarkable experiences and to feel special. They understand that these landmark experiences are delivered by precisely these value-added options. The innovators design their entire offering around putting their guests front and centre instead of selling room nights. The innovators thoughtfully design their offering to respond to their guests' desire to lead a well lifestyle. As a result, they deliver wellness experiences that are authentic, memorable and shareable – experiences their guests can't find at the hotel next door.

Myth 3: 'We're in the hospitality business, not the wellness business.'

The traditionalist's mindset

The traditionalists believe they are in the hospitality business and not the wellness business, and hence they opt for a third-party spa operator to manage their entire wellness offering for them. They avoid the liability of managing the spa and gym themselves (which for them constitutes their entire wellness offering) and of incurring the upkeep costs of such a complex business. Traditionalists have parts of their wellness offering run under a different brand to the hotel, with different brand values and a different vibe that don't match with the rest of their in-hotel experience. As a result, they deliver their guests substandard and fragmented experiences.

Myth buster: 'We're in the business of hospitality.'

The innovator's mindset

The innovators believe they are in the business of hospitality. For them, hospitality is about delivering their guests authentic, holistic and memorable experiences, and as innovative and forward-thinking hoteliers, their job is to ensure their guests live these landmark experiences. They control each part of their guests' journeys so that their guests live seamlessly perfect and integrated experiences. Just as Greggs didn't change its core business from bakery to vegan food specialist, the innovators don't change their core business from landmark experience providers to wellness gurus. Instead, as hospitality experts, they understand that wellness is an integral part of how they deliver their guests the landmark experiences they desire.

"

THE INNOVATORS SEE WELLNESS
AS THEIR OPPORTUNITY TO PIVOT
AND RESPOND TO CHANGING
MARKET CONDITIONS

"

FALSE ECONOMIES

Another common fallacy around wellness in hospitality is false economies. This fallacy leads the traditional hoteliers to stretch their resources too thinly, mistakenly thinking they're saving money. The Band-Aid solutions of this short-term strategy cost the business much more than the original cost of proper investment, alienating guests and denting the hotel's image in the process.

Myth 4: 'I practise wellness in my real life, so I know the wellness business.'

The traditionalist's mindset

Traditionalists who practise wellness in their own lives feel qualified to use these personal preferences as a benchmark and guiding principle when setting up their wellness offerings. They mistakenly believe their guests have the same wellness needs as they do and that they are looking for the same solutions. I remember one general manager of an all-inclusive luxury resort who was a triathlete and had trained for years. He thought that because he practised sport he knew how to restructure the gym, so he set it up according to his own training preferences. After several guest complaints, he realised the expensive way that the gym did not meet the training needs of guests on holiday in an exotic destination.

Myth buster: 'I practise wellness in my real life, so I know how complex wellness is.'

The innovator's mindset

The innovators realise that everyone is different, and so are their wellness needs. They might practise wellness in their day-to-day lives, but they understand that their wellness needs and wellbeing problems are personal and different from their ideal guests'. For them, it is what their guests want that matters, not what they as individuals want. They study their guests' wellness needs and design the right wellness offering to give their guests what they are looking for. Just as Greggs didn't create the vegan sausage roll based on their general manager's personal preferences, innovators don't design their wellness offerings based on their own likes and dislikes.

Myth 5: 'We don't need to pay for expert help – we can do it ourselves.'

The traditionalist's mindset

The traditionalists strive to streamline costs and optimise resources. To save money, they rely on the skill, expertise and experience of their in-house talent to design their wellness offering. They believe that if they have an experienced spa director, they will automatically make wellness successful, or that they can leverage the passion of their less knowledgeable staff to get by. They learn the hard way that wellness goes beyond their spa, and that passion alone can't replace expert know-how. By then, they have incurred more costs fixing their wellness offering than expert fees. A classic error is to have poorly designed facilities that negatively impact guest experience – for example, a treatment room next door to a children's play area.

Myth buster: 'If we don't pay for expert help, it'll cost us more later.'

The innovator's mindset

The innovators view their hotels as businesses with immense potential that deliver healthy returns on investment like few others. They think ahead and understand the importance of doing things right from the outset, and are unwilling to incur the substantial costs of doing things on the cheap. They pay for the necessary expert input to do things properly. They work together with their experts and take their time to create the right wellness concept; they don't jump into large investments, building facilities or creating offerings that won't work for their hotel. The innovators invest in developing the right system and processes so that their teams can do their jobs properly and deliver their guests the landmark experiences.

Myth 6: 'It's the therapists' job to sell wellness.'

The traditionalist's mindset

The traditionalists want their sales teams to focus on selling room nights and pushing groups, conferences and weddings. For them, it's the spa's job to sell wellness. They believe that, since the therapists aren't performing back-to-back treatments during their shift, they should make themselves useful and sell wellness in their downtime. Traditionalists have unhappy therapists who eventually leave because they are given tasks they don't enjoy or don't have the skills to perform – for example, standing in the lobby or outside the breakfast outlet to sell treatments. By trying to optimise resources, the traditionalists actually spend more in hiring and training new therapists, and they continue to struggle to sell wellness.

Myth buster: 'My sales team don't sell the hotel in bits and pieces; they sell the entire hotel.'

The innovator's mindset

The innovators view their hotel as one big ecosystem that comprises a number of different products, each equally important. They know that what makes them money is not one product, but the entire product ecosystem. Hence, their sales teams sell the whole ecosystem instead of picking and choosing parts of it. They also understand that sales is a specialist field and requires professionals who have experience. They place the right professionals in each position. They understand that their therapists' skill set and expertise lies in helping guests achieve their wellbeing goals by providing outstanding wellness experiences. The innovators have happy staff who do what they love to, happy guests who repeat their custom, and a hotel that reaches sales targets.

FALSE PROFITS

The last common fallacy around wellness in hospitality is false profits. This fallacy leads hoteliers to think they're making more profits, when in reality the gain in short-term profits comes at an opportunity cost in the long term. As a result, they fail to create a robust asset ecosystem because they focus on swift gains instead of solid and steady profits (the doomed asset-light approach we saw in Chapter 1).

Myth 7: 'It's a compensation tool, nothing more.'

The traditionalist's mindset

The traditionalists believe that, because hotels are people-centred businesses, service blunders and unhappy guests are inevitable. What matters, therefore, is not the blunder in service, but how their team manages the situation. Their strategy for attracting guests relies heavily on achieving high rankings on platforms such as Booking.com and TripAdvisor. Whenever there is an angry guest due to a broken shower or other service blunder, they believe it is more profitable to give a treatment for free instead of taking the risk of having their ranking pulled down by a negative review. However, their temporary solution for bad service eventually paves the way for much bigger losses.

Myth buster: 'I'd rather fix the problem than compensate angry guests.'

The innovator's mindset

The innovators pre-empt service blunders and unhappy guests by putting the necessary checks in place. They systematically correct and fix things that aren't working, so they never come to the point of making their guests angry and having to compensate them. For the innovators, offering guests freebies is putting a plaster on a festering wound that sets off a chain of incrementally harmful internal and external problems. Innovators believe that using a strong revenue generator like their wellness offering as a compensation tool is not good business practice and only devalues their asset ecosystem. As a result, they have happier teams and guests, and they enjoy solid returns on investment.

Myth 8: 'I'll just copy what they're doing – that'll bring guests in.'

The traditionalist's mindset

The traditionalists think they'll pull in more clients by copying what another seemingly successful hotel is doing with its wellness offering. They believe that if an offering is working for that hotel, it will magically work for theirs, too. They disregard the reality of the apparently similar hotel – its different owners, team, rules and regulations, target audience, and so on – and the way in which the differences impact the success of its wellness offering. They forget that the success of a concept in one hotel does not guarantee its success in another. The traditionalists get sidetracked by influencer predictions, shiny equipment and trending therapies, thinking these will help their wellness offering stand out and increase revenue.

Myth buster: 'What works there won't necessarily work here.'

The innovator's mindset

The innovators know it is their unique way of doing wellness in their hotel that differentiates them from the rest. The way in which they deliver wellness will attract a discerning guest who is willing to pay a premium for a quality wellness experience. They focus on making every guest's experience so special and memorable that guests want to share their experiences with their networks – a demographic that is similar to that of the hotel's ideal guest. The innovators have a loyal, committed and engaged following that promotes their hotel without being incentivised to do so. They create concepts that are authentic and integral to their asset ecosystem, and true to their essence; they don't borrow from others.

Myth 9: 'Wellness is not a big enough market.'

The traditionalist's mindset

The traditionalists build their entire property and offerings – hotel rooms, large conference rooms, small gym, several food and beverage outlets – around one predominant target audience: business travel. They make their property rigid and inflexible to changing market conditions by essentially positioning themselves as just another hotel with the same offering. When business travel came to a practical standstill during the 2020 pandemic, these hotels' bricks-and-mortar businesses came to a screeching halt overnight because they'd become over-reliant on a demographic that was previously very profitable but that has suddenly stopped buying. The traditionalists were left with facilities that were irrelevant or obsolete, prompting them to massively discount prices and to scrounge for the scarce available custom.

Myth buster: 'Wellness is the new corporate segment.'

The innovator's mindset

The innovators future-proof their hotels by diversifying their reach instead of becoming over-reliant on a decreasing market segment like business travel. They look at their guests' entire journey and consider the defining, key moments – from before their guests arrive to long after they have left – and they explore non-traditional revenue streams to continue to engage with their guests and sell more. Just as Greggs realised they could no longer be over-reliant on the decreasing meat-eating segment, the innovators recognise that if they don't respond to their increasingly wellness-conscious travellers' needs and pivot their business, they will soon become obsolete or have no place in the new normal.

PART 2
MY
APPROACH

'HOTELS ARE LANDMARKS IN THE COMMUNITIES THEY ARE IN. WHEN THEY FILL THEIR ROLE IN THE COMMUNITY WELL, THEY BRING IT TO LIFE, ALLOWING THE LOCAL CULTURE TO EXPRESS ITS HOSPITALITY AND AUTHENTICITY.'

- SONAL UBEROI

CHAPTER 3
MY STORY

HOW I GOT INTO WELLNESS

My story is part luck (being in the right place at the right time) and part deliberate pursuit (crafting the legacy I want to leave behind).

I was born and brought up in Kenya, where sport– particularly running– was an important part of the school curriculum. That training at school set me up for one day becoming a regular marathon runner, and that disciplined pursuit of a strong, resilient and healthy body is still very much a part of who I am.

I'm also from a spiritual culture, where Ayurveda, Vastu Shastra and holistic health are an integral part of life. When my mum's mum came to Kenya from India, a whole new world opened to me. I loved watching her make potions of herbs and spices for when we were ill or injured, and I distinctly remember her dedication to daily meditation – two hours, starting at 5am! Wellness was in my everyday life long before I came to realise it.

When it was time for me to choose a career path, wellness wasn't considered an industry in its own right, and there was no established career path available – even in the UK, where I went to study. So I went on to read law at university, as I figured an LLB Hons degree from a top law school would always be useful.

But I was still drawn heavily towards wellness. I was a fitness fanatic. Because London was prohibitively expensive for a student, I got myself a part-time job – in a health club, which allowed me to work out for free every day! I loved that job so much that I kept it long after I needed the money, when I had graduated and started to work at Goldman Sachs as a financial analyst.

At that point in my life, I was living the best of the two worlds I enjoyed. I loved my part-time job at the health club, where I was learning the ins and outs of operating a services business, from the bottom up. At the other extreme, I also loved being part of the City's buzz, and developing solid finance skills. I enjoyed learning the intricacies of business, investment and how economies worked, and I couldn't have found a better place to do it than one of the best investment firms in the world. I later realised how valuable these skills were.

By 2002, 'wellness' was beginning to boom in all its modalities (fitness, spa, nutrition etc.). It was becoming an industry in its own right, and it was then that I boldly decided to take the leap and leave Goldman Sachs to dedicate myself 100% to the world of wellness. You can imagine the reaction of utter shock I received from my loved ones, friends and colleagues. Why would anyone in their right mind want to leave the City's golden cage to work in a sports club in Madrid for less than half the salary?

My answer was simple: I wanted to spend every day of my life doing something I truly felt passionate about, while making a positive impact in people's lives. There was no better way to achieve that than by enhancing people's over-all wellbeing.

MARRIAGE OF BUSINESS ACUMEN AND PASSION

As I became more deeply immersed in the wellness world, I noticed that wellness professionals (therapists, personal trainers, physiotherapists etc.) were all fantastic at their chosen craft – they were true artists driven by a strong sense of purpose, each of them making a noticeable difference in their clients' lives – but they all seemed to lack the necessary business acumen to make their passion a financial success. With my financial analyst's background, I began to see a pattern to what was going wrong.

Wellness professionals are, by nature, sensitive, intuitive and connected people. You really can't be good at any of the specialities if you don't possess these innate characteristics. Most have spent thousands of dollars and several years on courses to further specialise in their fields, enabling them to help people in a more profound way; rarely, however, have they developed finance, business or management skills. They (and many hoteliers) mistakenly believe that being excellent at their craft will make them excellent wellness managers.

So when these wellness professionals work their way up to management positions, they find that, although they are familiar with their part of operations, they lack the necessary skills to manage multidisciplinary teams and suppliers, to develop sales and marketing plans and to analyse the business's profit and loss. They also lack the ability to take a wide, long-term view of the business to make effective strategic decisions.

At the other extreme, I came across strong professionals with proven track records from other sectors – but with little to no experience in the wellness field – come in and mistakenly think they could turn wellness businesses around by implementing best practices from other sectors. They, too, eventually failed to make their wellness operations generate optimal and sustainable revenues over the long term.

They'd suffer from high staff turnover due to low morale, or get seduced by whatever new wellness trend they thought would be the solution to the underperforming business. These professionals lacked knowledge of the nuances of the wellness business and how complicated it is to manage multidisciplinary teams who are not hardwired to think about business and operational efficiencies.

Neither of these extremes – great wellness professionals with no business skills, and great entrepreneurs with no real experience in wellness – enjoyed much success.

I found success at the crossroads of both worlds: business acumen and a deep knowledge of wellness. It is solid experience in the wellness field, combined with a wellness-oriented lifestyle and strong business acumen, that lead to stellar performance.

WHY HOSPITALITY?

I have always found hotels truly compelling, from the initial stages when they are little more than an idea and there is an excited rumour in the market that a new hotel is in the cooking, right to when there is a finished building, completely operational and the pride of the community.

Through my father, I was fortunate enough to get a glimpse into the process from scratch: the choice of site, submission of tenders, permit applications and breaking of grounds, and watching the building take shape over the months and years. I also had a glimpse into the not so glamorous parts, when things went wrong – unfortunate accidents on the building site, signed agreements with hotel operators falling through at the last minute, and situations that were beyond anyone's control (terror attacks, floods, riots… even coups d'état).

The most exciting part for me was always when the hotel operations team came on site and started bringing the hotel to life. I would watch them inhabit the building site, working up to the pre-opening frenzy, which continued until the doors opened. I distinctly remember the pride of everyone involved in making the hotel a reality – from design to operations – and their sheer joy during the launch event.

Several years later, and after working in the club in Madrid, I joined Six Senses Spas, where I was fortunate enough to

_ **"** _

WHEN WE THOUGHTFULLY AND
MEANINGFULLY CONSIDER
WELLNESS WITHIN ALL OUR GUEST
EXPERIENCES, THAT IS WHEN THE
MAGIC HAPPENS

_ **"** _

have the chance to truly appreciate the breadth of the hotel business from the inside – including the power of wellness in hospitality. I was fascinated by all the different professions involved, the sheer scale of the projects and the visible impact they had on their community. To this day, I marvel at the immensity of the hotel owner's task in raising the finance and shaping the property, and the general manager's skill in attracting and retaining customers, putting together a diverse team (sales, revenue, rooms, housekeeping, food and beverages, maintenance, wellness etc.), negotiating with suppliers, as well as keeping investors, public officials and the key stakeholders in the community happy.

Hotels are landmarks in their communities. When they fulfil their role in the community well, they bring it to life, allowing the local culture to express its hospitality and authenticity.

MERGING WELLNESS WITH HOSPITALITY

There is tremendous power at the intersection between hospitality and wellness. No other intersection of two industries has such power to profoundly and positively impact people.

When they are thoughtfully combined, the potential of these two industries to touch people in a truly unique and authentic way is immense. There is no better way of making a personal connection than allowing someone into your home and your world – letting them connect with the surroundings, discover new places, cultures, people, food, healing traditions and ways of living, and experience different realities.

When we thoughtfully and meaningfully consider wellness within all our guest experiences, that is when the magic happens. The healthy breakfast tailored to the needs and tastes of each guest, the ergonomic pillow and mattress to ensure a good night's sleep, the soothing scent to encourage relaxation, the surrounding vineyard to walk through or practise yoga in, the lovely massage to release those tensions, that amazing glass of wine, or simply the chance to laze around and do absolutely nothing while your children are being entertained– each of these small details contributes to our guests' wellbeing. Each and every detail impacts them in a profound way that makes them feel refreshed and energised, helping them to put their problems and worries into perspective so they can lead more fulfilling lives.

There is no better formula than combining wellness with hospitality to enhance overall wellbeing – of our guests, teams and environment, and of the surrounding community.

WHAT I'VE DONE

Over the last two decades, I have worked on more than 40 projects in 21 countries across Europe, the Americas, the Middle East, Asia-Pacific and Africa.

I've enjoyed seeing the wellness and hospitality industries grow and I've loved being part of these industries from different perspectives: from the bottom, learning the ins and outs of the operations of standalone facilities in different countries and cultures, being on the ground and spearheading the opening of the then largest spa in the Middle East, and from the top, in corporate regional and global positions. And lastly, setting up my own boutique consultancy and experiencing a completely different perspective and business reality.

I have successfully– and not so successfully– pitched wellness projects to owners from both perspectives: as the operator (backed by a fancy title, a solid corporate structure and the resources of a big hotel chain name) and as an independent consultant (myself, backed by my small, barely known company on a shoe-string budget). On each of these occasions, my strong business and finance background helped me put forward my case using solid arguments.

I've been at the top of the wellness chain, where I've worked for organisations that have viewed wellness as part of their DNA. I was fortunate to have learned from innovative and forward-thinking hoteliers how wellness can yield substantial returns on investment.

I've also been at the bottom of the wellness chain, working for larger, more traditional hotel chains for which wellness represented less than 1% of total company revenue, and naively believing that I, alone, could swim upstream and change things. I failed.

I've also registered my own fusion wellness concept – the Spa Sommelier concept (which I'll discuss later in Part 3) – and celebrated the huge success it has had in a landmark property in a region where wellness is not considered worthy of hoteliers' investment.

I have seen wellness work incredibly well; I have also seen wellness fail miserably, and felt despair at the missed opportunity. I know what works when hotels try to deliver wellness, and what does not. I've carefully combined what works into my ESSENCE model, which I will walk you through in Part 4.

MY LEGACY

History has shown time and again that the hospitality indus-try is very resilient. We have survived wars, terrorist attacks, natural disasters, economic crises and epidemics– even pandemics! We've been the first to be hit and the last to recover many times. But we've always bounced back stron-ger, ready to welcome our guests once again (who've always eagerly wanted to come back). However, we've never really needed to change what we've always done; the system worked, tourism boomed, and hotels mushroomed across the globe, yielding healthy returns on investment for their owners.

But this time round, things are different. We've never wit-nessed such a perfect storm, where entire countries went into lockdown, our businesses were thrown into near stand-still overnight on a global level and our main feeder market, business travel, was no longer buying from us.

So, the things that got us here will not get us to where we want to be – a strong position as an innovative and for-ward-thinking industry that has a positive impact on its people, community and environment. What will get us there is not reverting to a model based predominantly on business travel and corporate clients (a demographic that is no longer buying as it used to), but focusing on the true essence of hospitality– creating authentic, meaningful and memorable experiences. In other words: wellness.

This time round, we have the opportunity to truly take well-ness and hospitality to another level. There has never been a better time in history to be in both industries and to truly integrate them– to create landmarks of wellbeing that can change people's lives in a significant and meaningful way. People are increasingly buying into lifestyle choices, and we're perfectly positioned to ride the wellness wave.

I want to show hoteliers, even the sceptical ones, that wellness does indeed make business sense. And no matter how urban or mid-scale your property is, incorporating wellness into it in a meaningful and coherent way will yield substantial dividends. I can show you how as I walk you through my unique and carefully honed ESSENCE model.

I want to see this tribe of forward-thinking, audacious and innovative hoteliers leave their landmarks as a legacy for future generations. I want to join these hoteliers who are genuinely invested in enhancing the wellbeing of their community, guests, staff and investors. Together with this tribe, I want to take hospitality to another dimension that no other sector can achieve.

Above all, I believe wellness is for everyone. When I was growing up, people didn't have to leave home to find it. Today, it should be a toolkit that is available to all our guests walking through the door and aspiring to experience wellbeing.

If you want to be part of this tribe of hoteliers, let's connect on LinkedIn and continue the conversation: **www.linkedin.com/in/sonaluberoi/.**

CHAPTER 4
THE HARSH TRUTHS OF WELLNESS IN HOSPITALITY

B y now, you might be thinking to yourself that your wellness offering hasn't performed as well as you'd hoped. You might have a sense of where you may have gone wrong in your thinking, planning or implementation, perhaps due to lack of experience or challenging circumstances.

You may also have considered what you know about wellness and realised you have been working with certain misconceptions that have hindered your success with wellness or put you at a crossroads with your new wellness idea – for example, slipping back into your comfort zone when it came to the crunch, like one of my clients did.

My client, a hotel investment firm, acquired a once emblematic hotel in an affluent staycation region. Their mission was to turn around the property and offer something truly different: a wellness lifestyle hotel. They wanted it to be the first hotel in that region to make wellbeing an integral part of its DNA.

We wrote ambitious but achievable financial projections– 17% of total hotel revenue– for the new wellbeing centre, which would be a one-stop shop for our guests' wellness needs. We also put aside a reasonable budget to build such a facility.

As the project progressed, however, my client fell into the familiar hoteliers' trap: seduced by the potential for improving rooms, they lost sight of the initial project and substantially exceeded the building budget. As they had already started working on the rooms and the food and beverage areas, the only area where they could make noticeable cuts was the wellness facility, which was still in the blueprint phase. The easiest step was to cut the size of the facility, reducing the number of treatment rooms by nearly 40% and shrinking the fitness area, even though these areas were important direct and indirect revenue generators.

They believed they could streamline the size of the wellness facility and still make the same projected revenue by approaching their treatment room inventory in the same way as they did their hotel room inventory. In their minds, an average projected treatment room occupancy of 20% in year 1, working up to 65% in year 4, meant they could reduce the number of treatment rooms by 40% and still make roughly the same revenue. But they ignored the different revenue-generating models of the two areas; hotel rooms have a nightly revenue model, while spas have an hourly revenue model. The hourly and monthly subscription revenue models mean that a well-designed wellness facility can make a huge difference

"

THE HOURLY AND MONTHLY
SUBSCRIPTION REVENUE MODELS
MEAN THAT A WELL-DESIGNED
WELLNESS FACILITY CAN MAKE A
HUGE DIFFERENCE TO OVERALL
HOTEL REVENUE, PARTICULARLY IN
DESTINATIONS THAT SUFFER FROM
A FAIR AMOUNT OF SEASONALITY

"

to overall hotel revenue, particularly in destinations that suffer from a fair amount of seasonality.

A hotel can achieve near 100% occupancy for days on end in high season. A guest checks out by noon, and a new guest is occupying the same room by 3pm. But in a spa, you will rarely achieve 100% occupancy (yes, I've actually witnessed 100% treatment room occupancy, and I firmly advocate against it), and if you do, it'll only be on the odd day. Therapists need time to clean a treatment room and prepare for the next treatment (about 15 minutes on average in pre-pandemic times), and guests also need time to recompose themselves after their treatments. Hence, a treatment room (with its revenue-generating occupancy measured by the hour) will never reach 100% occupancy without compromising guest experience or staff wellbeing. The 100% equivalent would actually be 75% (accounting for the 15 minutes turnaround time needed for every 60-minute treatment) – and post-pandemic, we're probably looking at a maximum of about 60%.

Despite their reduced budget, my client was still easily seduced by flashy gadgets, happy to invest a substantial sum in a trendy piece of equipment that was still new to the market without considering its longevity. But they weren't prepared to invest in maintaining the initial treatment room inventory, which would actually generate more revenue in the long run.

What started out as a solid plan ended up being a muddled process that doomed the wellness centre to failure from the outset. It was clear that it would not generate the expected revenue and the rest of the hotel would have to compensate.

This client, like many traditional hoteliers, had genuine intentions to make wellness an integral part of this hotel's DNA, but they embarked on the journey without taking into account the 10 harsh truths about wellness in hospitality.

1. WELLNESS STARTS WITH YOU

No matter how grand your facilities or great your team, wellness will never work without the most important piece of the puzzle: you. You are the one who has to believe in wellness; you are the one who has to pitch the differentiating concept to your stakeholders and get their buy-in; you're the one who will need to put the systems in place, hire and train the right people, make your guests happy, and deliver your owners the return on investment you've promised. As soon as you accept that wellness starts with you, you adopt the right mindset and only bet on the wellness concept if you are truly willing to see it through to success.

2. WELLNESS IS AN ASSET

Wellness is both a tangible and an intangible asset. It increases the value of your hotel and attracts investors. It generates direct revenue through products and services, as well as indirect revenue through higher occupancy, average rate, average spend and length of stay – the tangible aspects of your business – as we saw in Myth 1 in Chapter 2. When done right, it also builds a stellar reputation for your hotel and fosters brand loyalty and trust with all stakeholders: guests, staff, suppliers, owners and investors – the intangible aspects of your business. As soon as you accept the tangible and intangible value of your wellness offering, you stop looking at the vanity metrics and focus on building your wellness asset and consolidating your asset ecosystem to increase its value and that of the entire hotel.

3. WELLNESS TAKES TIME

Wellness is not a quick-fix or Band-Aid solution to make up for dips in revenue. It's not like rooms or a restaurant, where a few good marketing and PR campaigns will suffice to fill them and generate weeks-long waiting lists. Fernando Gibaja, a seasoned hotelier, succinctly makes this point in his interview with me, and I'll share his case study in Part 4. Wellness takes time; it is a lifestyle choice, not a commodity. It is like a strong government bond that steadily and consistently grows in value over time, rather than suffering from drastic fluctuations in demand (like stocks do) and providing inconsistent and unpredictable returns. As soon as you understand that in order to build a landmark hotel using your wellness asset, it will require a longer incubation period than other areas of the hotel, you will stop looking for quick fixes or swift returns and instead focus on long-term growth.

4. WELLNESS ISN'T EASY

Wellness is hard. At the core of wellness, you are solving people's wellbeing problems that they can't solve themselves or don't know how to. That is actually what makes your wellness offering valuable. Beyond that, you face the challenges of developing the right concept, keeping owners happy, motivating and retaining your people, controlling costs and managing the daily grind of operations – all of this while dealing with the endless wellness facility maintenance issues without a deep knowledge of the wellness business. It's hard! As soon as you accept that wellness is not straightforward, you won't let the first setback make you write off your wellness offering as an underperformer.

5. THERE IS NO MAGIC FORMULA

There is no one particular treatment, machine, brand, professional or product that will magically generate the revenue and return you want your wellness offering to give you. It is the sum of the individual people, treatments, services, facilities and partners that make up your whole wellness offering that makes things happen. It is the entire ecosystem that makes wellness successful in your hotel. Once you accept that there is no magic formula when it comes to wellness, you stop chasing the newest trend, flashiest gadget or wellness guru and you concentrate on adding things that make the whole offering work better, instead of just hastily replacing parts of it.

6. WELLNESS CAN ONLY BE ACHIEVED THROUGH THE WELLNESS OF YOUR PEOPLE

Today, many employees have the option to work where they want and how they want, to create a sense of work–life balance. This is not the case for the hospitality industry, where staff face gruelling and antisocial hours that aren't conducive to wellbeing. Companies worldwide have been forced to genuinely integrate the wellbeing of their staff in their employment packages and working conditions to retain their talent. As soon as you accept that you can't solve your guests' wellbeing problems with a team that is 'unwell', you start to explore options to make your people's working hours more friendly and conducive to a balanced lifestyle that works for employees across different generations and different life situations. Heather Davis, a young and dynamic hotelier, rightfully advocates for staff wellbeing in my *Wellness in Hospitality* interview series. You can read the article here: **www.linkedin.com/pulse/wellness-hospitality-interview-heather-davis-sonal-uberoi/.**

7. YOUR GUESTS DON'T CARE ABOUT THE DEFINITION OF WELLNESS

As professionals of the industry, we waste too much time and energy worrying about how to define wellness and how we label our offering and features. We fret over what treatment and services constitute wellness, when all along our guests really don't care. They just want their wellbeing problems solved, irrespective of how we choose to define things. They won't stop having a massage because one day, as an industry, we decide it is no longer 'wellness'. As soon as you accept that your guests don't care how you define wellness, you start to focus on what really matters: the guest. You listen to your guest as you know they will tell you what they want.

8. WELLNESS IS CONSTANTLY EVOLVING

Wellness, as we know it, is a relatively new and rapidly growing industry. What was relevant a few years ago might not be important in three or four years' time, as became even more evident in the global pandemic; overnight, people began consuming wellness services in a very different way. As soon as you accept that some of your products and services will no longer be relevant to your guests, and that you will need to constantly innovate (they can be small tweaks), you won't feel disheartened when some of your offerings become irrelevant. Instead, you'll keep a strategic eye on how to improve your offering while keeping your guests' needs front and centre.

9. WELLNESS IS EVERYWHERE

Wellness is no longer confined to a specific activity or a physical space; real wellness is more than a spa, a gym or a studio. The definition of wellness is broad and involves anything that enhances overall wellbeing. Therefore, a lot of activities – such as horse riding, hiking in the mountains, cooking classes and coaching sessions, or wine tasting – that many hoteliers are already offering their guests are essentially wellness-related activities. Once you accept that you can't keep away from wellness – whether you have an urban hotel or a resort, whether you are budget, mid-scale or luxury – you start seeing the immense revenue-generating opportunity in front of you that wellness adds to your hotel offering.

10. WELLNESS IS DIVERSE

Wellness, like medicine, is a diverse field with a broad range of specialities. Just as we don't expect a general practitioner to be a specialist in every aspect of medicine, we can't expect a physiotherapist to know about beauty, or an energy healer to know about high-intensity interval training programmes. Once you accept that wellness is a diverse and specialist field, you will stop embarking on the mission impossible of trying to find a multi-skilled wellness team that knows how to perform all the treatments and services you offer. Just as you don't expect your sushi chef to jump in and cook dishes in your Indian restaurant, you won't expect your physiotherapist to jump in and perform pedicures.

Once you understand and accept these 10 harsh truths about wellness, you will open yourself to the opportunity to transform your wellness offering into a highly profitable and attractive asset for your business. In Part 3, I will show you how you can transform your business using wellness through my proven ESSENCE methodology.

PART 3
THE ESSENCE MODEL

'THERE WILL BE A MAJOR SHIFT WHEN THE OWNERS RECOGNISE THAT THIS [WELLNESS] ACTUALLY HAS VALUE-ADDED WHICH HAS A FINANCIAL MEANS TO IT, NOT JUST LOVELY IDEAS AND COMMUNICATIONS AND COLLATERALS BUT IN A BANK.'

- LASZLO PUCZKO

CHAPTER 5
INTRODUCTION TO THE ESSENCE MODEL

Does this sound familiar? You hire a great wellness director or a star therapist to turn your wellness business around. They highlight all the things you've been doing wrong and suggest changes that sound fantastic. You give them the go-ahead. Things seem great... but one day they leave, and so does your entire concept. I hear about cases like this all the time.

I designed my ESSENCE model to address the common pitfalls and to show hoteliers how to do wellness right and to make money while doing so.

WHAT IS IT?

My ESSENCE model is your fast track to profitability. It is a step-by-step process that shows hoteliers how to build a successful wellness offering – from a rough wellness idea to a profit-generating wellness asset.

It is a unique methodology that I created and honed over the years of working with not only some of the best hotel wellness projects in the world but also the box-standard ones. Many of these projects cost millions of dollars, but others were done on shoe-string budgets. I tested, tried and learned what works and what doesn't work with wellness in hospitality, and refined the things that work into a proven process.

There are seven key stages needed to make wellness work, irrespective of the type, size and segment of a hotel (new build, refurbishment or already operational). All these stages are pivotal in creating a solid wellness asset. When any of the stages are skipped, you end up with box-standard wellness offerings that underperform, are heavily subsidised, or bleed money.

When I work with my clients, I take them through the seven key stages of the ESSENCE model and show them how to create wellness offerings that work for their hotel's reality – wellness offerings that add value to the hotel's ecosystem without breaking budget or building facilities that become outdated before the investment is recouped, or that are part of brand standard but don't make business sense in that particular hotel.

In the next few chapters, I'll walk you through my unique ESSENCE methodology and show you how you, too, can deliver extraordinary results with ordinary tools and resources.

WHO DOES IT WORK FOR?

The ESSENCE model works best for hotels with a room inventory of between 20 and 120 rooms, whether they are budget, mid-scale, luxury, urban, resort or all-inclusive concepts. It provides hoteliers with the framework upon which they can develop their wellness asset and future-proof their business while not being led astray by the next big trend.

HOW DID IT COME ABOUT?

Frustrated by the missed opportunity with wellness, I was determined to find a way to make wellness in hospitality a lucrative business.

Over the years, I have seen several grand wellness concepts fail or become businesses that aren't profitable, while other simple concepts become successful and very profitable.

I have been part of projects where tens of thousands of dollars were spent in conducting detailed market research and feasibility studies, and creating brand stories and truly unique concepts. However, when it came to implementation, these wellness concepts never really enjoyed success or profitability, because certain key steps were not considered or were skipped entirely– for example, not costing offerings or carefully studying their upkeep costs, leading to facilities that never returned the amount invested in them.

I have also been part of projects where a modest investment was made in developing a simple yet authentic wellness concept, with the necessary market study and numbers, and these concepts later led to award-winning hotels, some of them the best hotels in their region. This is because they fol-

EVEN THE BEST OF IDEAS, WITH
GENEROUS FUNDING, CAN FAIL
EVENTUALLY IF THEY ARE NOT
IMPLEMENTED PROPERLY

lowed the ESSENCE principles, staying true to their concept and building a loyal and committed customer base.

Having a winning idea on its own does not suffice. Even the best of ideas, with generous funding, can fail eventually if they are not implemented properly. Conversely, even the very simple wellness ideas– ideas that aren't particularly innovative, spectacular or costly– can have tremendous success and be profitable if they get the ESSENCE principles right.

WHAT IS THE OUTCOME?

When you take your wellness idea through the ESSENCE model, you end up with a wellness offering that:

- Is authentic and relevant
- Generates healthy direct and indirect revenues
- Easily adapts and responds to changing market conditions
- Differentiates your hotel from the rest
- Future-proofs your hotel.

You have a happy, committed and motivated team because they are given the opportunity to shine. They have the framework and tools to craft and deliver landmark experiences.

You have happy guests who leave rave reviews and provide repeat business because their wellbeing problems are solved and they get to live their landmark experiences.

Your investors and owners are happy because they gain healthy returns on investment with your strategy. They trust you and are confident in your ability to create a performance-driven and customer-centric business.

Your hotel becomes a landmark within the community; it becomes a meaningful contributor in terms of not only the local economy and employment, but also the social and environmental wellbeing aspects of your wellness asset.

Your life becomes easier. Instead of constantly putting out fires, managing unhappy staff, and dealing with broken equipment, outdated facilities and angry guests, you can dedicate your time to the bigger picture, to the things you want and the things you enjoy doing. Above all, you have the time to craft your legacy in an intentional and meaningful way.

THE ESSENCE MODEL

How can you create a wellness asset that generates profits in the post-pandemic world? Here are the seven ESSENCE principles that show you the steps you can take right away to create a wellness concept that adds value to your hotel and helps you build a committed and loyal customer base.

Expectation

How do you know your wellness idea has potential and is realistic? By the end of Expectation, you will be confident that you have the right concept for your hotel, one that has been stress-tested, has true potential and is realistic to implement. You'll have a concept you can successfully pitch to owners and investors; you'll have a reliable gyroscope.

Story

How do you know your wellness idea solves your guests' real wellbeing problems? By the end of Story, you will have put your guests front and centre of your business. You will have created a winning plan to guide them through their journey to their wellbeing goal. You'll have successfully addressed their wellness needs.

System

How do you know your way of doing wellness is different from the rest? By the end of System, you will have created your special way of doing wellness in your hotel that is not vulnerable to the shifts and tilts of key personnel change. You'll have built a business that is systems-led, not people-led.

Execution

How do you know you have the right team to do wellness in your hotel? By the end of Execution, you will have successfully implemented your wellness concept without hiring staff you can't afford. You'll have a lean and ideal team – a team that aligns with your brand values and is confident, motivated and engaged.

Navigation

How do you know you're on track with your wellness concept? By the end of Navigation, you will have stayed on track with your wellness concept. You won't have been led astray by the newest trending therapy, flashy equipment or wellness guru. You will be aligned with your big-picture goals and your avatar's (ideal guest's) real wellness needs.

Consistency

How can you make sure you're delivering landmark experiences consistently? By the end of Consistency, you will have pre-empted service blunders caused by human error, guesswork and improvisation. You'll have put the right checks in place so your team can deliver your guests those landmark experiences, each and every time, without working harder.

Engagement

How do you know how loyal and committed your guests are to your brand? By the end of Engagement, you will have built a pipeline of customers and rave reviews through a loyal and committed customer base that genuinely engages with your brand long after they've left your hotel. You will have built a landmark in your destination.

THE ESSENCE MODEL IN ACTION

To illustrate how the ESSENCE model works, I will use the following two projects I worked on as case studies through each of the seven stages (the names and certain details of the hotels have been changed for privacy and confidentiality reasons):

CASE STUDY
(WHEN THINGS ARE DONE RIGHT)

HOTEL INNOVATOR

The property

Initially a 22-key resort with an expansion plan of eight new keys and a wellness facility, to take the total room inventory to 30 rooms.

The challenge

The hotel was in a remote location with little to do other than visiting wineries, which called for shorter stays, predominantly at weekends. The challenge was to convert the beautifully restored but empty hotel into a profitable business by tripling the average daily rate (ADR) and increasing the average spend per guest through the new wellness concept.

The approach

We followed the seven principles of the ESSENCE model. We ensured we had the right wellness concept that not only satisfied the owners but also addressed the wellness needs of their ideal guests. We created our special way of doing wellness that differentiated us from the rest (instead of introducing a trending therapy) and found local talent that we successfully trained up to deliver landmark experiences without breaking budget. Six months after opening, we had stayed true to our concept, despite temptation to add the latest gadget, but opted to fine-tune some details to better it. We made mistakes, but we put the right checks in place to avoid repeating them. And finally, we went the extra mile to curate special moments for our guests that they could easily share.

The outcome

Within the first year of launching the wellness concept, the hotel reached its target of tripling ADR and average spend, and doubling occupancy. It has been rated the best hotel in the Iberian Peninsula for several years in a row and enjoys a committed and loyal customer base that actively engages with the brand. The hotel is a landmark in the region and the country, and has changed the way wellness is done in luxury hotels in the Iberian Peninsula.

CASE STUDY
(WHEN THINGS ARE DONE WRONG)

HOTEL TRADITIONALIST

The property

Initially a 40-key resort with an expansion plan of six new keys and a wellness facility, to take the total room inventory to 46 rooms.

The challenge

The challenge was to develop a pioneering, sustainable wellness concept that delivered landmark experiences to both the early adopters and slow converters of the environmentally conscious way of living, and that generated a healthy return on investment instead of becoming an amenity to their overall concept.

The approach

The hotel skipped the first three principles of the ESSENCE model: stress-testing their wellness idea until they had the right wellness concept that satisfied both the owners and their guests, while creating their own special way of doing wellness.

As consumers of alternative therapies, the owners designed their wellness concept based on their wellbeing goals (remember Myth 4 in Chapter 2?) and hired expensive therapists to work their magic – but didn't show them what to do or how to do it. As a result, each professional did wellness in their own different way. This led to inconsistency in service and unhappy guests. To add to the confusion, the owners got sidetracked by trending therapies, implementing them without testing the market first, in the hope that they'd find the one treatment, product or brand that would solve their problem of low sales.

The outcome

The owners set themselves up for failure from the outset, having gone through several phases of trial and error, some incredibly costly, but none of them successful. They continue to be frustrated with their wellness offering as they can never quite get to grips with operations. As soon as they have a steady team and things seem to be going well, the star therapist leaves – and so does their new concept. Their wellness operation is a heavily subsidised amenity.

In the next few chapters, I'll share my proven and tested ESSENCE methodology so you can take steps right away that will make your wellness offering more successful and profitable.

Part 3 of the book is packed full of information, as I want you to get the most value out of this book. Keep your pencil, notebook and highlighter handy so you can make notes and highlight sections as you read along. To make things easier for you, I have also prepared my Wellness Business Essentials Toolkit, where you can download templates as you work through the exercises in each of the stages. You can access the Wellness Business Essentials Toolkit here **www.spa-balance.com/wellness-business-essentials-toolkit/** I'll prompt you along the way, so you know which templates to use when.

Before we dive into this transformational journey, you need to know where you are starting from, so if you haven't yet downloaded my ESSENCE scorecard, head over to **www.spa-balance.com/essence-scorecard/** and do so now. I'm going to be referring to your scores throughout the following chapters and you'll get the most out of this if you know where you are starting from.

Are you ready to become a forward-thinking hotelier and create a landmark wellness destination?

CHAPTER 6
EXPECTATION

There are two sides to consider when creating your wellness concept:

1. What you as a hotelier want to offer.

2. What your guests, as consumers of those services, want to consume.

In the first stage of the ESSENCE model, Expectation, we focus on you: on your side – what you as a hotelier want, and what you can offer that is truly unique and different from the hotel next door.

WHAT IS EXPECTATION ABOUT?

Expectation is about being certain you have the right, most profitable and practical wellness concept that you can present to your stakeholders with confidence. We work on your wellness idea and convert it into the right wellness offering for your hotel's reality and target audience, irrespective of the type of hotel or whether you have a new-build or an existing hotel, and irrespective of whether you're looking to add wellness into your offering or simply wanting to pivot an existing wellness concept.

We start by putting the pieces together; we study the different wellness ideas and choose the one that could work for your hotel. We then stress-test the idea to see what potential that wellness idea has and how realistically it could become an Asset.

In Expectation, we create the best wellness concept for your hotel (your gyroscope).

WHY IS EXPECTATION IMPORTANT?

The success of your wellness asset starts from this initial phase – getting the wellness idea right and converting it into a solid wellness concept for your hotel.

Expectation is important because it:

- Provides the foundation upon which the rest of your wellness asset is built

- Gives you reassurance and confidence that the concept is robust

- Brings clarity as to which wellness offerings would address your ideal guests' wellness needs

- Provides transparency in terms of cost of investing in the wellness concept and when you can realistically recoup your investment

- Prevents you from falling into the trap of the three fallacies we saw in Chapter 2: false perception, false economies and false profits

- Allows you to adopt a more strategic rather than a reactive approach to your wellness concept.

When you get Expectation wrong, you lack clear direction. You lack the confidence to successfully pitch your wellness concept to owners because, deep down, you aren't 100% sure that the concept you are pitching will guarantee a coherent return on investment. This lack of confidence filters down to other aspects of your business; for example, you struggle to attract quality talent who want to work with you, your guests aren't wowed and your owners don't fully trust your judgement as they can perceive the lack of clarity and confidence. In the end, you don't have a reliable gyroscope that will orient you towards your goal.

HOW DO YOU GET EXPECTATION RIGHT?

You do this in four parts. First, you define your wellness idea; second, you tweak it until you're happy with it; third, you stress-test it; and last, you modify it until you have a solid wellness concept for your hotel. Let's dive in.

1. Draft your wellness idea

You might already have a rough wellness idea or two, or you might not be sure what wellness services you could offer. A good starting point is to get back to the drawing board and to do the groundwork on your Who, What, Why and How.

Who is your ideal guest?

Define your ideal customer (your avatar).

- Who are they?

- What do they do?

- What age group do they belong to?

- What lifestyle do they lead?

- What are their motivations?

- What makes them tick?

- What are their wellness needs?

- What are their wellness services consumption habits?

- What are they willing to spend?

- What are their wellbeing aspirations?

Zero in on who your ideal guest is. Get to know them so well that you can paint a clear picture of who they are and what they like. Note that your ideal guest might not be your current guest, so think about who you actually want to attract and not who currently buys from you.

Invest in a professional market study that includes detailed customer surveys, targeted interviews, competitor analysis and market trends to get reliable, data-rich information so you can make informed decisions. Good market and feasibility studies are very specialised and time-consuming and require resources and a skill set that your sales and marketing or wellness directors– even wellness consultancy firms– are unlikely to have. The quality of the information you get from the market study, and thus the quality of the decisions you make, will depend heavily on the quality of the market study.

What can you offer them?

Now that you have reliable, data-rich information on your avatar (your ideal guest), what can you offer them to satisfy their wellness needs?

- What wellness services does this avatar buy from other hotels?

- What do they spend on them?

- If your hotel has an existing wellness offering, does it truly satisfy this demand? Are any services or facilities missing?

- If your hotel doesn't have a wellness offering, what kind of wellness options could you introduce?

Keep a close eye on the market. Know your competitors (direct and indirect) well. What are they offering? How are they offering it? What are they doing differently that is attracting your avatar?

In both cases, take a bird's eye view of your entire hotel offering, from rooms, food and beverage, and wellness to sporting and cultural activities in the destination. Paint with a broad brush. What could you include in your wellness offering that is both inside and outside your hotel? You are just mapping out potential ideas at this What stage – brainstorming different ideas and narrowing them down to about three options. In the next step, Why, you'll work out which one will be the best.

"

WHAT WORKS VERY WELL FOR ME
IS KEEPING IN MIND THE WORST
- AND BEST - CASE SCENARIOS,
NOT ONLY OF YOUR WELLNESS
OFFERING, BUT ALSO OF THE
ENTIRE HOTEL

"

TOP TIP 1

The offerings that make the most difference do not need to be fancy or costly. Sometimes it is a question of adding something simple like a yoga mat and a few fitness accessories in some of your hotel rooms, or getting a local personal trainer to create an early morning running club for your guests.

Why this particular offering?

Now that you have painted a clear picture of your avatar and have a few ideas of wellness offerings that would cater to their wellness needs, take each idea and ask yourself 'why this particular offering?' The answer to this question is value based. What value does this offering add to either your top or your bottom lines? What revenue (direct or indirect) can you expect from it? Are your numbers based on realistic metrics and historical data of your hotel?

Consider the following:

- What is the projected revenue of each component of the wellness offering?

- What investment is required (the sum is rarely zero)?

- Do you need to adapt or repurpose physical spaces?

- What expertise (internal and external) would you need?

- What are the running costs?

- What upkeep is required?

- What is your return on investment – it doesn't need to be financial – and when can you expect it?

It is normal to focus only on the top line. However, it's important to know what it entails to generate these numbers.

What works very well for me is keeping in mind the worst- and best-case scenarios, not only of your wellness offering, but also of the entire hotel. A good wellness concept generates healthy direct and indirect revenues through increases in occupancy, average length of stay, ADR and average spend (as we saw in Harsh Truth 2 in Chapter 4). When I work with my clients, I encourage them to look at the bigger picture and to consider the overall profit and loss. This avoids making their wellness offering an add-on or amenity department.

The worst-case scenario is when your alarm bells start ringing. It's when you need to get worried and ramp up your efforts – for example, when you go below the minimal sustainable point in your bottom line. How you manage to navigate through this critical situation will either take you further into the red or help you to pivot out successfully.

The best-case scenario indicates the highest possible revenue (direct and indirect) you can expect from that particular wellness offering. It helps you keep your feet on the ground.

It also prevents you from folding under owner pressure and writing unrealistic budgets when market conditions change.

Your Who, What and Why make the 'soft' aspects of your wellness concept. The next step, the How, is to do with the 'hard' aspects of your wellness concept: systems, facilities, expertise and management.

How are you going to achieve these numbers?

Once you have created your ideal, worst- and best-case scenarios of each wellness offering, how will you achieve these numbers?

- What do you need in order to implement your concept properly?

- Do you need to build a specific facility?

- Do you need additional space? If so, what does this space look like? How are you going to build it?

- What specific expertise do you need to get on board?

- How will you get the financing, and from where?

- Are you 100% confident that you have got the numbers right?

In my experience, the How is the root cause of potentially catastrophic results further down the line. It is where the cracks start to form that later compromise the success of the wellness concept. This is because many wellness concepts are under-costed. If you scored low in Expectation in the

ESSENCE scorecard, spend time on your How. It'll save you time, money and headache later down the road.

It can actually be quite difficult to get realistic numbers together as there are so many elements to your wellness concept; this is something I often help hotels with because, even with a great finance team, they can't necessarily see all the short-term and ongoing costs involved in a project, and understandably so. But it's crucial to have accurate numbers to make a proper and well-informed decision.

In the How, you get into the practical aspects of your project. How realistic is it to implement? At the end of How, you'll have narrowed down your options to one – the one that makes the most business sense for the whole of your hotel.

Now that you have worked on the Who, What, Why and How of your different ideas and chosen the one wellness concept that makes most business sense, it is time to stress-test it.

EXERCISE 1

CREATE YOUR WELLNESS CONCEPT

Narrow your rough ideas down to the one that makes most business sense for your hotel. This will be your working wellness concept.

Download my **Wellness Concept Value Canvas** from the Wellness Business Essentials Toolkit at **www.spa-balance. com/wellness-business-essentials-toolkit/** and let's dive in:

1. Take your different ideas and work on the Who and What of each of them.

2. Once you've worked on the Who and What, ask yourself Why this offering? Remember that the answer is value based, and don't forget your ideal, best- and worst-case scenarios.

3. Take your winning wellness idea and work on the How: how will you achieve the numbers you produced in Why?

You should have only one winning wellness idea at the end of this exercise.

2. Stress-test your wellness concept

You do this by using my Realisticity versus Potential graph.

What is the Realisticity versus Potential graph?

It is a measure that tells you the potential of your wellness concept and how realistic it is to implement.

I designed the Realisticity versus Potential graph because I've found it pivotal to consider both the realisticity and the potential of a wellness project. A wellness concept may be realistic to implement, but lack potential, or vice versa – it may have great potential, but not be very realistic to implement.

The potential of the wellness project is related to the 'soft' aspects of your business – your Who, What and Why (vision, mission and values). The realisticity of the project is related to the 'hard' aspect of the business – the How (the systems, expertise, facilities and management).

The graph below maps the realisticity of the project against its potential in four quadrants: Risk, Opportunity, Liability and Asset.

Risk

Concepts in Risk (bottom left quadrant) score low in both Realisticity and Potential. They are unrealistic to implement and don't have potential to become important revenue or value contributors. In many cases, they don't make business sense for the hotel to operate.

They lack the necessary 'hard' attributes (systems, staff, training and operational know-how) and the 'soft' attributes (purpose, vision and mission) to be successful. Wellness concepts that fall into this quadrant tend to be those that have been copied from another hotel (where they have seemingly been a success), or that are part of brand standards (e.g., a feature a luxury hotel must have) but neither the owner nor the hotel operator believes in its value or revenue-generation capacity. Success in these projects is rare.

You know your concept is a Risk if you have neither the soft aspects (your Who, What and Why) nor the hard aspects (the How).

Opportunity

Concepts in Opportunity (top left quadrant) have potential but are not very realistic to implement without being compromised.

Hotel wellness offerings in Opportunity have high revenue-generating potential in the long run. They have the necessary 'soft' aspects (a coherent vision, mission and well thought-out concept) but score low on Realisticity. The reason for this might be in your control (e.g., the concept requires talent that you currently have no access to but could acquire later) or not in your control (e.g., you might not have the physical space or funds to see your concept through without tweaking it).

You know your concept is an Opportunity if you have all the soft aspects in place (your Who, What and Why) but you don't have the necessary hard aspects (your How).

Liability

Concepts in Liability (bottom right quadrant) are realistic to implement but, in their current state, lack the potential to become an important revenue or value generator. In many cases, they generate losses.

Hotel wellness offerings that fall under Liability tend to either be those that the owner or general manager likes and wants to implement but without doing the groundwork, or those that have a nice spa facility. When an experienced spa director is on board, the spa is managed well and can generate satisfactory revenues. However, these hotels tend to lack an all-encompassing wellness concept that goes beyond the spa and they depend heavily on the skill of their spa director. When the spa director leaves, so does the entire concept and the spa's success quickly turns. Their wellness operations are treated as amenities rather than an integral part of the hotel experience; they usually represent about 1–3% of total hotel revenue and either barely break even, are heavily subsidised or bleed money.

You know your concept is a Liability if you have all the hard aspects in place (your How), but you haven't drilled down on your 'soft' aspects (your Who, What and Why).

Asset

Concepts in Asset (top right quadrant) rank high for both Realisticity and Potential. They have the potential to succeed and are realistic to implement.

They have a coherent vision that aligns with their avatar's wellness needs, and the right system, talent and management structure to consistently deliver landmark experiences. Concepts that fall under Asset are well planned, go beyond the spa and are seamlessly integrated into the hotel's essence. The perfect example of an Asset is Six Senses Resorts & Spas: in 2007, due to its wellness offering's high global recognition that reflected the lifestyle experiences offered at the resorts, the Evason brand was renamed, taking on its spa's brand identity.

You know your concept is an Asset when you have both the soft aspects (the Who, What and Why) and the hard aspects (the How).

How do you know if your wellness concept is a Risk, Opportunity, Liability or Asset? You stress-test it by checking how you measure in the soft and hard aspects on my Realisticity versus Potential graph.

How to stress-test your wellness concept

To stress-test your wellness concept, we start with Potential (the soft aspects of your concept), then move on to Realisticity (the hard aspects). I recommend you get other key stakeholders to stress-test the concept separately to check that you're aligned in your evaluations. It is actually quite common to get different results due to the different perspectives. If your answers are different, then sit down and discuss the points you are not aligned on. This will save you time, money and headache in the long run.

Potential (soft aspects):

Answer yes or no and then add the total points. Note: if it is not a clear 'yes', then mark 'no'. Yes = 1 point; No = 0 points.

	YES	NO
1. My entire team and I can clearly describe and are united on who our avatar is and what their wellness needs are.		
2. I know exactly what offerings will satisfy my avatar's wellness needs.		
3. I have invested in a professional market study.		
4. I know exactly how much money the concept will cost and what return on investment to expect.		
5. I'm confident that I can successfully pitch this wellness concept to stakeholders.		
Total number of points		

If you score between 0 and 2 points on Potential, your concept is either a Risk or a Liability.

If you score 3 points, your concept is either on the cusp of Risk and Opportunity, or on the cusp of Liability and Asset, depending on its Realisticity.

If you score between 4 and 5 points, well done. You either have an Opportunity or an Asset.

Now that you know where you score on the Potential of your wellness concept, you can move on to see how it measures on Realisticity.

Realisticity (hard aspects):

Answer yes or no and then add the total points. Note: if it is not a clear 'yes', then mark 'no'. Yes = 1 point; No = 0 points.

	YES	NO
1. I have, or can raise, the funds to create, implement and manage this wellness concept.		
2. I have, or can hire, the right expertise to create, implement and manage this wellness concept.		
3. I have, or can build, the spaces needed for the wellness concept.		
4. My hotel is ideally located for this wellness offering.		
5. I'm confident I can deliver the target return on investment with this wellness concept.		
Total number of points		

If you score between 0 and 2 points on Realisticity, your concept is a Risk or an Opportunity.

If you score 3 points, your concept is either on the cusp of Risk and Liability, or on the cusp of Opportunity and Asset, depending on its Potential.

If you score between 4 and 5 points, you either have a Liability or an Asset.

To find out exactly which quadrant your concept falls under, plot the total number of points under the hard and soft aspects onto the graph. You can download a completed example in my Wellness Business Essentials Toolkit here **www.spa-balance.com/wellness-business-essentials-toolkit/.**

If your concept falls under Risk, Opportunity or Liability, it's perfectly fine. This is actually quite normal for the first versions; you'll rarely get your concept right the first time. Concepts that fall under Asset have been modified several times beforehand.

EXERCISE 2
STRESS-TEST YOUR CONCEPT

Ensure your wellness concept is solid. You do that by understanding its true potential and how realistic it is to implement.

Open the Concept Stress-test Canvas from the Wellness Business Essentials Toolkit and let's dive in:

1. Start with the Potential of your wellness concept and answer 'Yes' or 'No' to the five criteria. Remember, if it isn't a clear 'Yes', then it's a 'No'.

2. Now work on the Realisticity of your wellness concept and answer 'Yes' or 'No' to the five criteria. Again, if it isn't a clear 'Yes', then it's a 'No'.

3. Modify and fine-tune your wellness concept

You get your wellness concept in the Asset quadrant by scoring a minimum of four points on both its Potential (the soft aspects) and its Realisticity (the hard aspects). It is generally relatively straightforward to improve your concept's potential, so this stage of Expectation is where you tweak the soft aspects you scored low on. Here's how.

Potential

Criterion 1: My entire team and I can clearly describe who our avatar is and what their wellness needs are

If you answered 'No', go back to the Who section and drill down on who your ideal guest (your avatar) is and what their wellness needs are. Involve your team in the process. Invite your owner and other stakeholders to the brainstorming sessions, to ensure you are all on the same page and clear about who your avatar is, what lifestyles they lead, what wellness services they consume, and so on. I usually moderate the discussion to encourage the sharing of those small details we can sometimes miss when we aren't in each other's shoes.

Criterion 2: I know exactly what offerings will satisfy my avatar's wellness needs

If you marked 'No', revisit the What section. What wellness services does your avatar consume in other hotels? What are other hotels (within and outside your comp set) doing differently? Involve your key heads of department and take a bird's eye view of your entire hotel, its surroundings and the local community. What does your hotel have that is truly unique and that your avatar wants? Many hoteliers struggle to see the uniqueness of their hotel objectively; it's sometimes the small gestures that make a big difference. Remember to paint with a broad brush.

Criterion 3: I have invested in a professional market study

If you haven't already done so, it is time to make that investment (from a specialist company, not a wellness consultancy firm that provides this service as an add-on). You need reliable, data-rich information to make the right decisions and to save you time, energy and money in the long run. There is only so much information you and your team can get on your own, and your time and skill set will be better employed in doing what you are supposed to do: creating a truly unique wellness offering based on reliable information instead of personal preferences.

Criterion 4: I know exactly how much money the concept will cost and what return on investment to expect

If you aren't crystal clear on this, revisit the Why section. Dive deep into the numbers of each component of the wellness offering, and research what the standard wellness service mix is in hotels. This is my area of speciality, because although finance teams are great at producing budgets, they need expert input on the intricacies of the wellness business. The idea is to leave no stone unturned when it comes to costings, maintenance and revenue. Continue with the exercise until you can answer 'Yes'. This stage takes time.

Criterion 5: I'm confident that I can successfully pitch this wellness concept to stakeholders

If you answered 'No', revisit criteria 1–4 until you feel confident. Pitching your concept is about showing its true potential and convincing your stakeholders. You are more likely to get people behind you when you truly believe in your concept's potential, and this is what the Who, What and Why sections give you. Keep your audience in mind; the same pitch will not work for all stakeholders. Consider who needs to hear what, their potential pushback and how you could respond to them. Most objections are due to lack of understanding or a lack of reliable information to inspire confidence in the concept.

Now that you have worked on the Potential of your wellness concept and have managed to score 4 or 5 points on it, I'll show you how to make your concept more realistic to implement – how you can improve the hard aspects.

Realisticity

Criterion 1: I have, or can raise, the funds to create, implement and manage this wellness concept

Finance tends to be the deciding factor for most projects. If you don't have, or can't raise, the necessary finance, revisit your What and Why. Does your wellness offering include any expensive equipment? Can you solve your avatar's problem with an equally effective but more affordable option? Look through each of your offerings and see how you can optimise resources. Then tweak your Why. When it comes to budgetary restraints, many hoteliers whittle down the What but not the Why, leaving financial projections unchanged. You do not do yourself or your team any favours if you hold yourselves to unrealistic expectations. Adjust your top and bottom lines to match your modified concept.

Criterion 2: I have the right expertise to create, implement and manage this wellness concept

If you answered 'No', this is relatively easier to fix than the first criterion. Identify where you lack the necessary expertise and reach out to your network to find professionals who have that experience in your type of hotel and offering. If you don't know where to start, this is an area I can help with. Many hoteliers hire professionals they don't need while cutting back on areas they can't afford to lose, because they lack in-depth knowledge of wellness operations. Having the right professionals early on in the project will save you time and money in the long run.

Criterion 3: I have, or can build, the spaces needed for the wellness concept

Lack of space tends to be another deciding factor. If you answered 'No', consider how you can repurpose other areas in your hotel. These spaces can be simple, but they must also be functional, inviting, and easy to access. Many hoteliers try to revive dead spaces (e.g., old back-of-house areas or the basement) by shoehorning wellness facilities into them, only to realise they have created another under-utilised and unappealing space. Another option is to look outside your hotel – who has facilities that you could use? Can you partner with them?

Criterion 4: My hotel is ideally located for this wellness concept

Location tends to be another deciding factor. If your hotel's wellness concept is not relevant to the destination – for example, a detox clinic in a party town – then it is unlikely to succeed without tremendous effort. How your destination promotes itself impacts the type of wellness concept you can implement. I'm not saying you can't be a game-changer, but swimming upstream requires a longer incubation period before the project takes off – I've known cases where it has taken over 10 years. Make your wellness concept relevant to the destination and your avatar. It will save you the uphill struggle and get you a swifter return on investment. Dhiren Pereira tackles location relevance brilliantly in my *Wellness in Hospitality* interview series. You can read the article here: **www.linkedin.com/pulse/wellness-hospitality-interview-dhiren-pereira-sonal-uberoi.**

Criterion 5: I'm confident I can make a success of this wellness concept

If you aren't confident, revisit criteria 1–4. Is your lack of confidence because you can't raise the necessary funds? Is it because you can't afford the right talent? Or is it a question of space or location? Look at what factors are within your control and how you can adapt your wellness concept to fit the reality of your hotel.

When working on projects, I ask myself 'will they be able to make this wellness concept a continued success five to seven years down the line?' Only once I can confidently answer 'Yes' do I know I have the right wellness concept for that particular project.

TOP TIP 2

Ask yourself the question 'can this wellness concept be a continued success five to seven years down the line?' Only once you can confidently answer 'Yes' do you know you have the right wellness concept for your hotel.

Unlike the Potential of your wellness concept, you will notice it is harder to score 4 or 5 points on its Realisticity. Some factors, like financing and space, tend to be decisive and are often beyond your control. This is why most hoteliers end up with amenity concepts that provide a service to the guest, but do not stand out from those of the hotel next door.

EXERCISE 3

MAKE YOUR CONCEPT AN ASSET

Invest the time and resources into making your wellness concept an Asset.

Open the Gyroscope Canvas from the Wellness Business Essentials Toolkit and let's dive in.

1. Just as you did when you were stress-testing your concept, work on Potential first. Revisit criteria 1–5 on Potential until you score a minimum of four points.

2. Now revisit criteria 1–5 on Realisticity until you score a minimum of four points. Remember, this section is slightly tougher than Potential. Take your time.

CASE STUDIES

Let's take a look at the two case studies and see the Expectation stage in action. In our examples, Hotel Innovator followed the principles outlined in Expectation and moved their wellness concept from Risk to Asset, despite it involving a pivot and delay in the project to prevent substantial losses. Hotel Traditionalist ended up with a chaotic project because the owners insisted their concept was the right one despite it being on the cusp of Liability and Risk; they weren't willing to slow down, re-evaluate and open doors late for fear of missing the high season.

CASE STUDY
(WHEN THINGS ARE DONE RIGHT)

HOTEL INNOVATOR

The challenge

The owners hired a top spa consultant to create a world-class spa concept, and she delivered. She created a beautiful, grand themed spa concept spreading over 3,000 square metres, making it one of its kind in the region – which they loved. Although the new general manager liked the concept (it was difficult not to), the challenge was to convince the owners to put the project on hold until they got a second opinion, because the projected investment was substantial. They reached out to me.

The approach

The themed spa concept scored high on Realisticity (4 points), but low on Potential (1 point). The project had the funds and the physical space, making the concept realistic to implement, but it lacked some key soft aspects. When I drilled down into the Who, I saw the offering didn't appeal to the right customer; the What similarly wasn't offering what their ideal customers wanted; and when I looked at the numbers in Why, I could see that this very expensive project had been seriously under-costed. Where the owners could only see a stunning spa, I could see red flags. Although the concept was beautiful, grand and new in the region, it was essentially a huge risk.

When I shared my serious concerns, the general manager and owners decided they were not prepared to take on the huge risk and potential monumental losses. They agreed to modify the concept, even if it led to an important pivot in the project and caused delays. The numbers showed that even with the costs of essentially starting from scratch and the delay in opening it, the additional expenses and potential loss in revenue were substantially lower than the losses they would incur in making the wrong investment decision.

We set out to modify the concept. From the professional market study, we learned that our avatar would not fly in from, for example, Brazil to one of the best wine regions in Spain to experience something they could get at a fine hotel in Asia. They wanted to get something out of their stay in this hotel that they hadn't got before and couldn't find anywhere else.

We took a bird's eye view of the entire hotel and its breathtaking surroundings and looked at which wellness-related activities could be integrated into the hotel's overall offering to create authentic and memorable experiences for our guests. We modified the concept until it fell under Asset.

The outcome

The result of modifying the concept from Risk to Asset was the Spa Sommelier concept. The Spa Sommelier is my registered fusion wellness concept inspired by master sommeliers and traditional Chinese medicine's Five Elements Theory. A master sommelier has detailed knowledge of terroir, the wines' qualities, and the foods and tastes the wines can be paired with. The Five Elements theory shows us how the structures and systems in our bodies are connected to each other, and how we are connected to our environment and surroundings.

This inspired me to create the figure of the Spa Sommelier, whose role was to design and craft authentic wellness experiences that paired together local flavours and hotel spaces with each guest's wellness needs while connecting them with the breathtaking surroundings. You can learn more about the concept at **www.spa-sommelier.com.**

Not only was Spa Sommelier unique and a big hit– generating the hotel four times more in indirect revenue through increased ADR, occupancy, length of stay, average spend and repeat custom– but it also saved the hotel thousands of dollars in build out (1,200 square metres versus 3,000 square metres for a 30-key hotel), equipment, upkeep and staffing costs.

The hotel had a clearly defined gyroscope – a reliable compass to keep all stakeholders on track and prevent them from getting drawn into offerings that would bleed money. It was upon this clarity, firm ground and confidence that the next stages of the project were built.

Hotel Innovator's example demonstrates that you do not need a grand or costly concept to truly stand out. A winning concept for you could actually be very simple and easy to implement– provided you've stress-tested and modified it until it's an Asset. The Expectation part of the process ensures you have a sensible concept before you jump into investing large sums on something that might not be successful or profitable because it is not relevant to your hotel or destination. It provides you with a reliable gyroscope to keep you on the right track. You'll see its relevance as we work through the next stages.

In the next case study, I show you how a wellness concept that falls under 'Risk', 'Liability' or 'Opportunity' is rarely successful unless it is modified to 'Asset'.

CASE STUDY
(WHEN THINGS ARE DONE WRONG)

HOTEL TRADITIONALIST

The challenge

The owners appointed their personal healer as the wellness director. As consumers of alternative therapies, they believed they already knew what to do. They had a clear vision of their sustainable wellness concept (an eco-spa and gym).

The general manager admired the young couple's vision and determination, but he was also wary of the fact that neither they nor the healer had experience in creating and operating such a concept. His big challenge was getting his owners aligned with the reality of their wellness concept.

The approach

When we stress-tested it, the general manager and I found the concept to be a Liability and the owners a Risk. Although on the surface the difference between Risk and Liability might seem small, the discrepancy in results was worrying. All businesses pose a risk, to a certain degree; however, there is a big difference between a Liability and a Risk. A Liability means you will not recoup your investment and the business will always be a cost and drain on your resources, generating losses and causing distress. A Risk means you're hedging your bets, but there is a possibility that you could succeed if you play your cards right– if you are lucky, you might make your investment back.

The hotel general manager was concerned about this lack of alignment, and he knew he had an uphill battle to make the owners see that their wellness concept was not an all-encompassing one and that it needed to be modified before it could be implemented. The Who was defined by customers who had the same likes and dislikes as the owners, the What was based on the popular hotel spa in the region, the Why used numbers from a famous retreat in Asia– and they skipped the costings phase altogether.

Eventually, the hotel general manager gave in to the desires of the owners, despite not being confident about the wellness concept. He was new, so he saw their passion and drive and thought perhaps they knew something I, the wellness business expert, didn't. He would later learn that this was a mistake – one that caused him several problems down the road as he battled with the wellness offering. He learned that if you don't challenge your owners when they're making bad decisions, you will be the one left picking up the pieces.

The outcome

Each person worked from a different perspective based on their own interpretation of what the wellness offering should be. This caused delays and disagreement at every step of the way. The end result was chaos, uncertainty and parties locking horns. The cost of coming up with Band-Aid solutions that didn't work and putting out constant fires was substantially higher than the cost of stopping the project and taking the necessary time to modify the concept from Liability to Asset.

Hotel Traditionalist's example demonstrates that passion and vision aren't enough to create a successful wellness concept. The owners were so committed to their vision that they relied on their passion to take their wellness idea and convert it into a concept without doing the necessary due diligence. They weren't prepared to tweak their concept for fear of changing it to one they weren't keen on, even though it was a liability and the modified concept made more business sense and was more aligned to their ideal guest's wellbeing needs. These passionate and well-intentioned owners failed to create a reliable gyroscope to guide them and keep them on track. It was upon this unreliable base that they implemented their entire wellness concept. In the next stages, we'll see how things went from bad to worse as a consequence.

CONCLUSION

It may be your passion, vision and experience that drive you to make your hotel truly unique and different from the rest, but it is your gyroscope that gets you (and keeps you) on the right track. However, it is your drive and love for hospitality that keeps things going. A hotel without such a leader is soulless. Traditional hoteliers use this deep passion as a fuel to tirelessly work behind the scenes, making themselves available 24 hours a day, seven days a week and (in many cases) 365 days a year, so that their guests can have the best possible experience in their hotel. They bend over backwards to keep guests happy, but in doing so, they unwittingly push their teams in different directions.

Innovative and forward-thinking general managers accept they need to juggle several different roles and please every stakeholder, but they also know the importance of having a gyroscope – a clearly defined destination and a carefully planned yet flexible roadmap that will get them there. They know that without this direction, they would be thrown into chaos and be forced to manage reactively to reach budget, and as a result, their guests and staff would be unhappy. They use their gyroscope to get all their stakeholders – their guests, teams, suppliers and owners, and themselves – aligned and on the same page, and reassuringly keep everyone on track. They don't waste their time constantly pulling everyone back on track. They manage from a place of clarity, confidence and authority.

KEY TAKE-HOMES

1. Even the grandest concepts can fail if they do not adapt to the unique realities of your hotel.

2. Know your Who (your ideal client), your What (your wellness offering), your Why (why this concept and not another) and your How (how you will implement your wellness concept).

3. Work on the ideal, best- and worst-case scenarios of your wellness concept to know what range of performance you can expect to work within.

4. Do you have a Risk, an Opportunity, a Liability or an Asset? Stress-test your concept to know its potential and how realistic it is to implement.

5. Modify and tweak your concept until it falls on the Asset quadrant. Once your concept is in the Asset quadrant, you know you have a reliable gyroscope to move forward.

CHAPTER 7
STORY

In the second stage of the ESSENCE model, Story, we focus on your guest's side of the wellness concept – what your ideal guest will feel in your hotel as they go through their wellness journey.

WHAT IS STORY ABOUT?

Story is about your avatar– your ideal guest. It's about putting yourself in their shoes and feeling the whole experience as they would feel it. In other words, it's their story, not yours.

How will they feel when they experience a wellness service in your hotel? Are things made easy for them? Are the different wellness-related areas near to one another? Can they have the services they want when they want and without any fuss? What are the potential obstacles to them achieving their wellbeing goals? Are their wellness needs being met? These are some of the questions we look at to shift your focus from what is convenient for the hotel to what is convenient for your guests– two different perspectives.

In Story, we create the winning plan that will enable you to successfully solve your guests' wellbeing problems.

WHY IS STORY IMPORTANT?

Today's consumers want to relate to and connect with a brand that aligns with their values and purpose. They set out to live authentic and memorable experiences through the brand; they want to tell their own unique story.

Now, more than ever, the basics of storytelling are essential to businesses. People respond to stories that resonate with them, stories that are relevant to their lives. Story is important because it:

- Allows you to look at your concept from your avatar's (your ideal guest's) perspective and offer them what they're looking for

- Helps you to clearly define your avatar's journey through your hotel and thus personalise their experience

- Shifts your focus from selling room nights to solving your avatar's wellbeing problems

- Prevents you from thinking about the next on-trend treatment or shiny piece of equipment to stand out in the noisy market

- Puts your avatar front and centre of your business and prevents stakeholders from using subjective decision-making.

When you get Story wrong, you unwittingly set yourself up for failure. You fail to see your offering from your customer's perspective and, as a consequence, you don't truly understand what they want, need or like. The biggest mistake brands make (not just hotels) is that they think about what they want to sell, not what the market wants or needs. This means they're more prone to adopt a reactive approach of trial and error in the hope of stumbling upon something their customers truly want.

HOW DO YOU GET STORY RIGHT?

A great story is one that connects with your avatar and makes them engage with your brand in a meaningful way. This happens when your avatar feels that the brand really knows and understands them and their problems. The only way to create such a great story is to make your avatar the front and centre of it.

This might sound easy; however, it is actually not that straightforward. It requires us to literally go against our grain. We are used to looking at things from our perspective; in fact, that is precisely what we did in Expectation. We want to make our hotel the best, we want to have that special 'wow' feature no other hotel has, we want a healthy return on investment – at the end of the day, we're all about us (which is OK and normal). We aren't used to putting our guests' shoes on and looking back at ourselves afresh. We aren't used to putting the consumer hat on when it comes to a business we know so well. This objectivity is hard, because we inevitably bring our beliefs, justifications, likes, dislikes and excuses to the table. How can our guests not want the great things we offer?

Storytelling is a powerful tool that helps us position our-selves where we can successfully make our guest the front and centre of the story, while also indirectly shining the spot-light on ourselves.

Before we delve into how we can use storytelling to help us achieve our ultimate goal, it is important to understand the basics of it. According to Donald Miller, author of *Building a StoryBrand*, there are seven main elements that make up a story:

1. The hero
2. The problem
3. The villain
4. The prize
5. The guide
6. The journey
7. The plan

But what have storytelling and its seven elements got to do with your hotel? You must be wondering: *hero, villain and guide – does it matter?* It matters a lot. You are not the hero of the story– your ideal guest is. Understanding the key roles and where you fit in the bigger picture (the story) is what will make or break your wellness concept. It's an area I work on closely with my clients, because many hoteliers struggle with the Story stage.

Let's take a look at the seven elements.

The hero

Every story needs a hero. One of the three main characters, the story is centred on them and their journey to the ultimate destination (the prize). In your hotel's story, your avatar (your ideal guest) is the hero.

Your avatars are the ones who are on a mission to get the prize. They are the ones who pay to live that experience. It is for them that you have set up the hotel (the stage and the plot). And everyone wants the hero to win; no one likes a story where the hero loses in the end.

However, hotels often make themselves the hero of their story by crafting their offering around their own needs and objectives – what makes it easy for them to sell their core business: room nights. So absorbed are they in being the best hotel and getting a handsome return on their investment that they wrongfully compete with their avatar for the hero spot. In the end, no one wins – neither the guest who is meant to be the hero, nor the hotel that accidentally takes the wrong role.

The problem

The hero has a deep problem that causes them serious pain and compromises their sense of wellbeing. This deep problem is a sum of different types of issues – physical, emotional, mental and existential – but to them, it's one big, nagging problem causing them pain, either literally or figuratively.

The problem is the reason they come to your hotel in the first place. They come to get rid of their pain, even if only temporarily. They do not come to your hotel for the fancy room, the grand chandelier, the Olympic-sized pool, the Michelin-star restaurant or the cryotherapy chamber the Real Madrid football team uses. They come to escape from the daily grind of life, to relax, to spend uninterrupted quality time with their loved ones, to get their head straight and reflect, or simply to spoil themselves for a change.

However, hotels accidentally create more problems for the guest by designing the experience badly; for example, guests encountering noisy treatment rooms or a leaking gymnasium, having to walk past the bar in their robe and slippers to get to the spa, or staring at a Kinesis machine and trying to figure out how it works.

The villain

No story is complete without a villain – the second of the three main characters. The villain brings problem after problem to the hero, making it difficult for the hero to get to their prize.

By competing for the hero's spot in the story, hotels accidentally become yet another villain in the hero's way. They become the bad guy, creating obstacles that hurt the hero (and the hotel, too!) and detonating another set of problems the hero didn't have before.

Becoming a villain is clearly not our intention; we want to make our guests happy, make them feel at home and show them a good time. We want to show them what true hospitality is about. But unfortunately, we get absorbed in thinking about what we want to offer, about creating the grandest and most unique concept while making healthy profits.

And without realising it, we forget to stop and see things from the perspective of the very people we want to make happy. Instead of guiding the hero smoothly on their journey to the prize, we ruin the story for everyone.

The prize

The prize is the end destination. It is the story's holy grail; in your hotel, it is the authentic, shareable, and memorable experiences– the landmark experiences– that your guests seek.

The prize consists of more than the traditional hospitable welcome and grand facilities. Your guests want to make the spaces they occupy as personal to them as possible. They want their deep problem to go away and they want to feel happy and enriched by their stay at your hotel. And that's precisely what you want, too. You want your guests to feel at home and make every corner of the hotel theirs. You want them to discover all the wonderful things your hotel, its people and the surroundings have to offer. You want them to live experiences they will remember for many years to come. You want to make them happier. The prize is what both you and your guest ultimately want.

You can see how perfectly things could work in an ideal world, and you want to offer what the guests want. However, the reality is different. Instead, we think we know what our guests want and we create our wellness offering based on that false premise.

The guide

The guide is the third main character. Every hero needs a guide, someone of immense wisdom, experience and intelligence who helps them along their journey to attain the prize. The guide is someone the hero trusts and who has some sort of authority that inspires confidence in the hero. They aren't (and don't need to be) perfect, but they know what they are doing.

In your story, the guide is your hotel. Positioning your hotel as the guide is a sure-fire way to future-proof your business and tap into a more discerning clientele that is willing to fully commit to embarking on the journey with the guide to the end destination – and spend more.

Hotels compete for the hero role, thinking it is the main spotlight to be under. However, it's actually the guide who plays the pivotal role in the story; it is the guide who makes it possible for the hero to reach their prize, who has the knowledge, wisdom and power to take the vulnerable hero on a memorable journey to the end destination. It is the guide's plan that lets the hero achieve victory. The guide is essentially the determining role.

The journey

The journey is a voyage the hero and the guide embark on together. You and your guests are in this together, albeit in different lanes. And you both want this journey to be enjoyable, authentic and memorable.

However, the journey isn't always as enjoyable as we all would like it to be, because we miscalculate when the journey actually starts and when it ends. Most hoteliers think the journey begins when the guest checks in to the hotel and ends when they check out. They overlook the most important parts of the journey: the pre-arrival and the post-departure.

It is during these all-important first and last moments when your guest truly connects with your hotel – and when they experience the highest levels of stress. It is in these parts of the journey that you have the greatest flexibility to be distinctively creative.

The journey doesn't have to be smooth; the path of the journey can wind, but you can still get your heroes to the endpoint, despite unexpected obstacles that are beyond your control (like a global pandemic), provided you do not step into villain mode and create your own obstacles along the way.

The plan

The plan is the guide's winning strategy that gets the hero to their prize. It is the carefully devised but malleable roadmap to the holy grail.

The pandemic made us acutely aware of how vulnerable the predominantly bricks-and-mortar business model of hotels was. When over 70% of hotels worldwide were forced to close their doors, they didn't know how to interact with their guests apart from hosting free virtual sessions on social platforms. Some managed to tap into the takeaway dining options of their restaurants, but the majority were forced to near zero revenue. This was because their whole plan – their entire product ecosystem – was built on one part of the journey: the guest's physical presence in the hotel. When guests couldn't physically come to the hotel, their reason to interact with the brand ceased.

A cleverly devised plan separates the hotels that do well from the ones that don't. The plan is where you essentially build in resilience, problem solving and innovative thinking. It doesn't matter if you can't physically open the doors, because your winning plan will still allow you to get your guest to their endpoint – that landmark experience.

Through storytelling, we have seen that the prize is the memorable landmark experience, which is what your avatar actually wants (and not what you think they want), but it's also what you want to deliver. In an ideal world, the hero (your avatar) and the guide (your hotel) are journeying towards this destination (the landmark experience) together. External to the hotel, there is a villain (stressful lifestyle, lack of work–life balance, no time etc.) bringing problem after problem upon the hero (e.g., migraines, tight back and shoulders, stress, depression) that cause the hero deep pain and make it difficult for them to obtain the landmark experience. They therefore reach out to the guide (your hotel), this wise and experienced figure, to solve their problems. The guide carefully devises the winning plan that ensures the hero will get their prize. End of story, and everyone lives happily ever after.

However, we have seen that in the real world, hotels unwittingly step into the villain's role when they try to make themselves, instead of their guests, the hero of the story. This catastrophe can be avoided if we understand that our role is essentially that of the guide, helping the real heroes to get to the end destination. The only way we can step into the guide role is by understanding the identity of our guests' real villain, who is causing them so many problems.

HOW DO YOU BECOME THE GUIDE OF THE STORY?

You do this in three parts:

1. Brainstorm your avatar's main villains and the well-being problems they cause.

2. Map out your avatar's entire journey through your hotel.

3. Study how you can guide your avatars through their journey and make a plan to help them reach their wellbeing goals.

1. Brainstorm your avatar's main villains and the wellbeing problems they cause

When it comes to your wellness offering, your avatars are not buying a massage, a personal training session, a healthy meal or any other wellness service. They are ultimately paying to solve a wellbeing problem – for example, to relax, de-stress, or alleviate the pain of a tight back.

When you talk about your guests' wellbeing problems, they begin to feel that you understand them and so they identify with your brand and hotel. To do that, you need to know who their villain is. What is the root cause of these wellbeing problems? Their villain is related to their big-picture lifestyle choice, whether that's as an executive with a C-suite job in a FTSE 100 company or a full-time homemaker and primary caregiver of three children.

Once you know who your avatar's main villains are, the next step is to identify the wellbeing problems they are causing your avatar. Most of your avatar's wellbeing problems fall under the following four categories:

Physical wellbeing problems

These are the problems your avatar suffers at a physical level – for example, headaches, tight shoulders, bad back or fatigue – and they can be directly or indirectly caused by the villain. Perhaps your guest has a stressful job with long hours, which means not having time to buy fresh food to cook themselves, or a demanding office job that means spending several hours crouched in front of a computer, causing bad posture and headaches.

Most hotel wellness offerings focus on solving these physical problems by, for example, offering deep tissue massage to remedy a tight back or an anti-ageing facial to make the skin more radiant. This is because, traditionally, most wellness businesses are built around offering short-term reprieve; it is the area they feel comfortable to operate in. These services offer instant, albeit temporary, relief. Who doesn't feel better after a massage?

But these physical problems tend to be symptoms of larger underlying lifestyle issues which aren't so easy to fix with a one-off treatment. By focusing on treating the symptom and offering temporary relief, these hotel wellness offerings build short-term and transient custom, instead of obtaining long-term and continuous custom by targeting the root cause.

Emotional wellbeing problems

These are the problems your avatar experiences at an emotional level – for example, anger, fear or frustration – and they can be directly or indirectly caused by the villain. For example, your guest may have a precarious job environment, which means they fear losing their job and not being able to meet obligations, or a stressful job with long hours, which means not having time to spend with their loved ones, causing family disharmony.

The rise of the experiential economy has led many hotels to heavily focus their offering on providing short-term reprieves from these emotional problems. But like the physical wellbeing problems, these emotional wellbeing problems are a symptom of a bigger issue. For the avatar with a stressful job, that great holiday with their family might temporarily remedy the family disharmony, but if the bigger problem isn't addressed, they'll remain on a constant lookout for another paradisiacal holiday to mend things, temporarily again.

Centring your wellness offering around solving emotional problems is a tall order. When you strive to offer that serendipitous 'wow' experience your guests have never lived before, you end up competing in a crowded and saturated market. It isn't a smart long-term strategy.

Mental wellbeing problems

These are the problems that affect your avatar psychologically. They build up over time and become pressing or chronic– for example, depression, insomnia and other mental health disorders– and they are mostly caused indirectly by the villain.

Going back to our avatar with a stressful job suffering from family disharmony, prolonged tension on their home front may eventually cause depression. This mental wellbeing problem will now need several coaching sessions to fix. Once your avatar finds the right professional, they are unlikely to change their choice until they feel better. It is this kind of continuity you are looking for– a relationship that goes beyond the physical realms of your hotel and past the bricks-and-mortar business model.

Very few hotels focus on solving mental wellbeing problems, because it tends to be a grey and taboo topic. They don't want to be labelled a hotel that 'specialises in mental health'– they can't offer luxury, promise paradise and wow guests, while at the same time offering services that make people work on themselves and feel worse before they feel better.

But you don't need to be a mental wellness hotel to offer these wellness services, because they can be packaged and marketed in a more inviting way. For example, you could offer online consultations with the world's best life coaches, or cooking workshops (perhaps online) with your executive chef to make quick, delicious and healthy dishes with foods that make your avatar feel better. These activities impact your avatar's mental wellbeing and are services you can offer at your hotel without jeopardising its luxury status.

It is in this niche set of problems that you have the greatest opportunity to make a noticeable and meaningful difference in your avatars' lives. It is the problem category that is most likely to get you repeat custom from a committed and loyal client base. Imagine if pre-pandemic hoteliers had built their wellness offerings around solving these mental health problems? They would have been well positioned to

"

HELPING YOUR GUESTS SOLVE
THEIR LONGER-TERM EXISTENTIAL
WELLBEING PROBLEMS WILL
LENGTHEN THE JOURNEY YOU
(THE GUIDE) AND YOUR AVATAR
(THE HERO) EMBARK ON.

"

tap into alternative streams of revenue that didn't require in-hotel presence.

Existential wellbeing problems

These are essentially spiritual wellbeing problems. They relate to one's inner self, life purpose or reason for being. Examples include: lack of clear direction in life, being at a crossroads, having a feeling of emptiness. They are mainly caused indirectly by the villain and slowly creep up on your avatar over time, and they aren't easy or quick to fix.

Referring back to our avatar with a stressful job, perhaps the further strain caused by the depression on their relationship with their spouse eventually leads to a separation. Although they've always loved their job, they now suddenly find themselves lost and without purpose. Most avatars at this stage consume long-term holistic therapies to find their bearings again.

Over the last 15 years, an increasing number of hotels have begun to offer holistic therapies to guide their guests through their existential wellbeing problems. The increased awareness of holistic therapies (e.g., naturopathy, Ayurveda, meditation, energy healing) and the increase in qualified specialists and visiting practitioners has made it easier for hotels to offer such services. Helping your guests solve their longer-term existential wellbeing problems will lengthen the journey you (the guide) and your avatar (the hero) embark on.

TOP TIP 3

The more niche and long-term the problems you solve, the more you'll connect and engage with your avatar (your ideal guest).

After working with me, my clients understand the importance of focusing on the niche, long-term problems. When you go niche, it keeps you focused and helps you tighten your wellness offering. Remember, you can't be everything to everyone.

If you scored low on Story in the ESSENCE scorecard, take your time to thoroughly work through your avatar's journey and to understand their longer-term wellbeing problems.

EXERCISE 4

UNDERSTAND YOUR AVATAR

Find out what your avatar's wellbeing problems are.

Download the Understand Your Avatar Canvas from the Wellness Business Essentials Toolkit at **www.spa-balance. com/wellness-business-essentials-toolkit/** and let's dive in:

1. Sit down with your team and brainstorm your avatar's main villain.

2. Identify at least 100 wellbeing problems that this villain causes your avatar.

3. Organise these 100 problems into the four categories: physical, mental, emotional and existential. Narrow them down to about three main wellbeing problems per category. These are the wellbeing problems you are aiming to help your avatar solve.

Now you have got your avatar's villain and wellbeing problems clear, the next step is to look at your avatar's journey and how you can help solve these problems.

2. Map out your avatar's entire journey through your hotel

Most hotels tend to focus on the part of the journey their guests spend in their hotel. They forget that their guests' on-property presence is actually only a part of their journey. Their journey begins long before they get to our property, from the moment they choose our hotel over the one next door; it involves the anticipation, the extra work they have completed before going on holiday, the organising of the logistics of the trip (what types of transportation they use to get to your hotel, flight delays etc.) and what needs to be done at home while they're on holiday (e.g., asking people to water their plants, look after their mascots).

Similarly, their journey does not end as soon as they have checked out from your hotel, but continues long afterwards. Your guests have to go through the same process they followed to get to your hotel – taking all the different types of transportation back to their home (and deal with any delays, noisy children, lost baggage etc.), getting back to work and playing catch-up on the backlog, and returning to the routine of the daily grind – but this time, they're taken from a place of relaxation to one with a high level of stress almost straightaway. All these factors that stress your client impact their overall wellbeing and undo the benefits of the wellness services they consumed at your hotel. Most people have long forgotten their holiday within a month of returning to work.

When you map out your avatar's journey, look at their entire journey through your hotel, from before they arrive to a time when they've long since left the premises. Mark each and every touchpoint where your team can guide your avatars to the next step in their journey. Remember that you are looking beyond your wellness team. You are looking at the entire hotel team: sales, reservations, guest services, reception, food and beverage, housekeeping, maintenance, and so on.

At this stage, you don't need to fret over who is going to do what; you are just identifying the opportunities along the journey where you could be your guest's guide. Paint with a broad brush, but also be specific. You are not trying to solve all your guests' wellbeing problems, only the dozen or so you listed above in Exercise 4.

Once you have defined the detailed journey of your guests, from before they get to your hotel until long after they leave, and have identified key touchpoints where your hotel can appear as the guide to solve a specific type of problem that your wellness offering specialises in, the next step is to come up with the winning plan to your avatar's prize.

EXERCISE 5

SIMULATE YOUR AVATAR'S JOURNEY

Map out your avatar's entire journey with your hotel, from pre-arrival to post-departure.

Open the Avatar's Journey Canvas from the Wellness Business Essentials Toolkit and let's dive in:

1. Sit down with your team and map out your avatar's entire journey, from before they get to your hotel to long after they leave.

2. Mark each and every touchpoint where your team can guide your avatar to the next step in their journey. This could be when they're booking their room, when they're making their travel arrangements, the actual trip to the hotel, check-in, the first moment they get to their room, and so on.

3. Study how you can guide your avatars through their journey and make a plan to help them reach their wellbeing goals

The purpose of drafting the winning plan at this stage of your wellness concept is two-fold:

1. **To build trust with your avatar.** Your avatar will trust you if they can sense your entire team knows what they are doing, that they know the plan.

2. **To bring clarity to the process.** Your entire team will know what they are doing if they have a clear plan to follow.

Pull together the main problems under the four categories you listed, along with the journey you mapped out, with the key touchpoints where your team could act as guides to your avatar, and now write down the plan for how your guides will help the hero along the way. Write out the road-map, clearly marking each milestone and what your team (as the guides) will need to do, and what your guest (the hero) will need to do to reach their wellbeing goal.

TOP TIP 4

The winning plan does not need to be complicated or grand. It can be simple, clear and easy to follow, with only a few key steps.

Your winning plan should detail the steps your guests need to take to look after themselves. For example, you could direct them to download a guided meditation session with your visiting practitioner pre-arrival, then when they're in your hotel, provide them with a note reminding them to stay hydrated after their long trip or to book a hydrothermal circuit so they can gently unwind. When they've left your hotel, they can subscribe to your daily wellbeing blog and receive tips on how to continue their wellness journey, join your hotel's wellness Facebook group to interact with other guests and be part of the community, or join a live session on how to avoid increasing stress levels.

These small, simple steps aren't costly, but they establish trust with your guest and make your team feel confident as everyone is clear on what the plan is. They also help to foster a sense of commitment from both your avatar (as they have the opportunity to create a lasting relationship that goes beyond their actual stay at the hotel) and your team (as they know what to do, when to do it, why they're doing it and how it will benefit the avatar).

Once we truly understand our guests' problems and the journey they're on, we have the opportunity to stand out and separate ourselves from the hotel next door. Our secret weapon is our unique plan, our creative strategy where we've built in resilience, problem solving, innovative thinking and flexibility.

EXERCISE 6
WRITE THE WINNING PLAN

It is in the winning plan where you and your team can get very creative.

Open the Winning Plan Canvas from the Wellness Business Essentials Toolkit and let's dive in:

1. Take your Avatar's Journey Canvas from Exercise 5 and, together with your team, brainstorm how you can help your avatar with their pain points at each of these touchpoints.

2. Start to write the master winning plan. Narrow down the ideas you brainstormed with your team to one option per touchpoint. Make sure each stage of the plan flows. For example, in the pre-arrival phase you might send guests a series of three emails with wellness tips that are relevant to their wellbeing problem; when they get to your hotel, you have a wellbeing goodie bag waiting for them; later that evening at turndown you have a sleep easy tea by their bedside; and so on.

CASE STUDIES

Let's take a look at the two case studies and see the Story stage in action, where Hotel Innovator followed the principles and positioned itself as the guide, and Hotel Traditionalist skipped the Story stage and positioned itself as the hero, unwittingly becoming the villain.

CASE STUDY
(WHEN THINGS ARE DONE RIGHT)

HOTEL INNOVATOR

The challenge

One of the avatars was an affluent, busy businessperson who travelled frequently – a 'bleisure' guest mixing business with leisure, while trying to stay healthy, jam-packing activities in the tail end or in between trips. Their villain was a fast-paced and high-profile lifestyle that caused them several wellbeing problems.

From Expectation, we knew the wellness offering we wanted to implement (the Spa Sommelier concept). The challenge was to align our wellness concept with what our avatar wanted to buy.

The approach

We gave each character the right role in the Story: the avatar as the hero, and the hotel as the guide. To understand our avatar's pain points, we brainstormed the wellbeing problems their high-profile, high-stress lifestyle was causing. We grouped these problems under the four categories (physical, emotional, mental and existential). Below is a rough sketch of the most important wellbeing problems we came up with after the exhaustive brainstorm:

PHYSICAL	EMOTIONAL	MENTAL	EXISTENTIAL
- Insufficient exercise - Uncomfort-able, stiff body - Dull, grey skin	- Anger - Frustration - Distress	- Anxiety - Insomnia - Impatience	- Lack of purpose - Confusion - Indifference

Because our primary goal was to create a loyal customer base, we opted to focus on their mental wellbeing problems. We mapped out our avatar's journey (ensuring we included the all-important pre-arrival and post-departure moments) and marked the key touchpoints along the way where we could have a meaningful impact so that we could create the winning plan.

In the pre-arrival and post-departure stages, a well-organised, hassle-free trip to and from the hotel was instrumental in reducing the client's overall stress. The hotel was remote, and the nearest international airport was over 200 kilometres away. Once at the airport, guests had a 20-minute taxi ride to the train station, an hour's high-speed train ride and another 40-minute taxi journey to the hotel. We could not change our guests' journey time, but we could control their experience and contribute to their overall wellbeing by reducing the stress associated with their travel. We signed leasing agreements with local luxury car companies to pick guests up at the airport and take them straight to the hotel, saving them the unnecessary headache and stress of taking the various transportations available. We included energy drinks, tasty but healthy snacks, water and scented towels in the cars, as well as free Wi-Fi access, so that guests were comfortable and could continue working while they were en route.

The outcome

The Spa Sommelier concept we created in Expectation was aligned with our avatar's longer-term wellbeing goals. The hotel's focus shifted from offering what they wanted to offer, to solving guests' wellbeing problems. It was no longer about what treatment, service or product to sell, but about what service, product or gesture would solve the guests' mental wellbeing problems (or at least prevent them getting worse). We had succeeded in putting the guests front and centre of their story; we now had a robust wellness concept ready to implement.

CASE STUDY
(WHEN THINGS ARE DONE WRONG)

HOTEL TRADITIONALIST

The challenge

The hotel team came to Story without a reliable gyroscope to orient them. The wellness concept was based on the wellness services the owners consumed and which their wellness guru thought interesting (her line of work), instead of data-driven research. The challenge was two-fold: firstly, to try to align the personal preferences each stakeholder (the hotel general manager, the wellness guru and the owners) had for the eco-spa concept with what their loosely defined avatars wanted to buy; and secondly, managing the amount of say each party had in shaping the wellness concept.

The approach

The owners fell into the trap of making themselves the hero of the story. They thought of the services each one of them would like and mixed their wants and desires as owners with the ones they held as wellness consumers, in their minds creating their dream wellness offering and landmark experience, and essentially falling victim to Myth 4 in Chapter 2.

They focused on making their experience as special as possible until they reached their landmark experience – each one different from the others– instead of thinking about what wellbeing problems they were solving with each offering. They weren't able to see the key touchpoints of the journey from the point of view of someone walking into their hotel for the first time. As a result, guests who came to the hotel didn't know that the hotel had a wellness offering, and when they did discover the spa, they didn't understand the services menu. For example, some guests would book for a Feldenkrais session but would leave disappointed, as what they were looking for was a standard massage that would help relieve their tight back.

Many guests didn't share the same sustainability vision as the hotel owners and, as a result, expected treatments and services that delivered instant results. For example, guests who had an anti-ageing facial expected more visible results. But because the products were natural and homemade – the therapists sometimes experimented with ingredients from the vegetable garden – they didn't deliver the results the guests had expected. Nor were the scents of the smashed natural fruit conducive to a sensorial experience. The guests wanted facials that produced instant results, and it didn't matter to them whether the products used were natural or not.

By making the story about them, the hotel accidentally created another set of problems for their guests that they didn't have when they came to the hotel.

The outcome

There was a battle of wills as each stakeholder fought for the prized hero position. This led to further tension and friction between them. Costs increased substantially as each stakeholder incorporated the products and services they wanted. But their guests' wellbeing needs continued to go unresolved while they faced new problems from the hotel (bookings getting cancelled, severe delays in treatments, facilities that didn't work etc.). At the same time, staff were confused and stressed as they continued to make mistakes and annoy their guests. In the end, the hotel had unwittingly become the villain of the story.

CONCLUSION

If it is the hero of the story– your avatar– who triumphs in the end, it is the guide, your hotel, that makes it possible for them to get their prize: the landmark experience. Traditional hoteliers step into the unpopular role of villain when they try to make themselves the hero of the story. They offer their guests what they think their guests want rather than what they actually want. This creates more problems for their guests and teams, because the guests don't want the things that are on offer and the teams don't know how to solve their problems. The traditional hoteliers make their job even more challenging as they find themselves dealing with unhappy clients, an unappealing offering, disengaged staff and dissatisfied owners.

Innovative and forward-thinking hoteliers get their aligned teams to journey together with their guests and guide them to their prize. They look beyond the physical hotel and seek to solve their guests' actual wellbeing problems, offering them the solutions they want. These hoteliers listen to their guests and truly understand their problems. Their teams feel happy, confident and fulfilled, because they solve their guests' wellbeing problems and deliver them the landmark experiences they want. They create a more committed and loyal following (their guests, your team and your owners) because they remove the battle of wills between stakeholders and, instead, become the leader everyone happily follows.

KEY TAKE-HOMES

1. The hero of the story is your avatar, your ideal client (who might not be your actual guest).

2. The hero already has a villain in their life: a bigger lifestyle problem that is setting off a series of pain points (wellbeing problems) they're looking to solve so they can get to their prize, the landmark experience.

3. The hero (your avatar) and the wise guide (your hotel) are journeying together to the same end destination: the prize.

4. The guide's carefully devised plan gets the hero to the prize by overcoming the problem. It is this smart and unique plan that makes your wellness concept watertight.

5. The innovative and forward-thinking hoteliers consciously place themselves as the guide instead of unwittingly becoming another villain who inflicts a different series of problems upon the hero.

CHAPTER 8
SYSTEM

The first two stages of the ESSENCE model dealt with creating the right wellness concept for your hotel. Expectation looked at the wellness concept from your (the hotelier's) point of view and gave you a reliable gyroscope to keep you and your team on track. Story looked at your wellness concept from your guest's point of view and provided you with the winning plan to guide your guest, the hero, as you journey together to the prized end destination: the memorable landmark experience.

The next two stages, System and Execution, are about how to smoothly and successfully implement your wellness concept.

In this chapter, I'll walk you through the third stage of the model: System.

WHAT IS SYSTEM ABOUT?

System is about creating the framework of your wellness concept, the foundation upon which you begin the implementation process. In this stage, we define how you do wellness in your hotel. It is about carefully evaluating how you can solve your avatar's wellbeing problems effectively while maintaining control of the business. It is about making your and your team's lives easier so that you don't need to improvise or make things up on the fly. It is about creating order, standardisation and discipline from the outset.

Your system is your proprietary way of delivering the carefully devised plan you created for the hero (your avatar) in Story – it is your 'trademark' way of solving your guests' wellbeing problems.

In System, we create your special way of doing wellness in your hotel.

WHY IS SYSTEM IMPORTANT?

No matter how talented or experienced your team are, they– and in turn, your business– will not succeed if you do not have the right system in place. Your system produces the results, your people manage the system. It is your system, your special way of doing things, that differentiates your hotel from the one next door.

System is important because it:

- Gives your avatar confidence in your hotel and that you know what you are doing – you solve their wellbeing problems and deliver the landmark experiences

- Helps you choose the right talent, people who are willing to learn and do things according to your proprietary way of doing wellness

"

NO MATTER HOW TALENTED OR
EXPERIENCED YOUR TEAM ARE,
THEY – AND IN TURN, YOUR
BUSINESS – WILL NOT SUCCEED
IF YOU DO NOT HAVE THE RIGHT
SYSTEM IN PLACE

"

- Brings clarity and structure; it sets you and your team up for success

- Frees your team from worrying about how to do things

- Removes subjective decision-making, guesswork and improvisation from the guest experience

- Integrates all the elements required to make your business run smoothly.

When you get System wrong, your wellness offering is vulnerable to the shifts and tilts of key personnel change. Each new general manager or wellness director will make changes in the wellness offering to match their personal preferences or past experiences– for example, replacing the product brand partner, redesigning the treatment menu, or hiring and firing staff. All these lead to an increase in costs, and the investment is often not recouped during the general manager's or wellness director's tenure at the hotel.

HOW DO YOU GET SYSTEM RIGHT?

Most hoteliers leave aside the details of their operating system until the operations team comes on board, at which point department heads are expected to write their own systems and processes.

However, that is a false premise. Your staff do not need to own your hotel's system – you do. It's your staff's job to make it work and to deliver landmark experiences to your guests, not to rewrite protocols or to own the system.

Your system and processes are put in place precisely to avoid subjective decision-making and to ensure consistency in operations, product, quality, customer service and the delivery of wellness experiences. When you allow your staff to adapt the system to their personal preferences, you actually make their job harder. If you scored low on System in the ESSENCE scorecard, reconsider your approach to your system and processes. Are you truly making your team's job easier?

GOLDEN RULES FOR YOUR SYSTEM

Hospitality is a mature industry with an established structure – which it has followed for decades – and a set of standard operating procedures for each department: rooms, food and beverage, purchasing, sales and finance. Over the last couple of decades, spa and fitness have been added, reporting directly to the rooms division in most cases. However, very few hotels have the systems in place for wellness throughout the client's journey.

Wellness is a diverse field including (but not limited to) spa, gym, mind–body activities and in-room fitness. A successful operating system brings these activities together in a holistic way, clearly shows your team how to deliver the landmark experiences, and is agile enough to adapt to changing market conditions.

I'd like to share the three golden rules for your system.

1. It must provide great value to all your stake-holders

Creating a system just for the sake of having one is neither helpful nor useful. Your system must provide great perceived value to everyone who interacts with your hotel: your guests, your owners, your team, the local community, your suppliers and any other person or business your hotel works with, either directly or indirectly. They must all see the value in following your system. In other words, your system must either make their lives easier or solve their problems.

You make your stakeholders' lives easier when your system – your proprietary way of doing things – tells them how you do business and when it reflects your hotel's core values, mission and vision. For example, you might want to offer culturally immersive wellness experiences where your guests have the opportunity to visit a local healer or shaman; for your system and processes to be useful and of value, they must show each stakeholder how these experiences are delivered from start to finish – from how the services are marketed to how your guest gets to the shaman and how the shaman provides the service. Your system must provide all the details so that nothing is left to guesswork and improvisation.

When your system makes your stakeholders' lives easier and doesn't create unnecessary problems, your stakeholders will want to follow it, because they will see the value in doing things the right way. It will also make your life easier, as operations will flow smoothly; you won't need to battle with pushback or put out unnecessary fires.

2. It should be operable by people with the lowest level of skill

TOP TIP 5

Build your system so that it is operable by staff with the lowest level of skill. If your system depends on highly skilled people, it's going to be very difficult to replicate.

This might sound counterintuitive to most hoteliers (and probably most businesses), because all industries advocate for qualified and skilled people. However, the major problem with this approach is that if your system depends on highly skilled people, it's going to be very difficult, if not impossible, to replicate. Most wellness and hospitality businesses battle tirelessly to hire and retain talent because they keep looking for the most qualified, experienced and skilled people. But it is not their expert skill that ensures the success of your business; it is the efficacy of your system. I'm not saying that qualified people or skill aren't important— they're very important, because it's your people who bring your system to life– but I am saying you need to create a system that is watertight.

As Michael E Gerber stated: 'Great businesses are not built by extraordinary people, but by ordinary people doing extraordinary things.' The only way ordinary people can do extraordinary things is if they have a great system that shows them how to do those extraordinary things – a system that sets them up for success.

When you make your hotel systems-dependent instead of people-dependent, you protect your wellness concept from being subject to the whims, moods and discretion of your staff. You avoid your wellness concept falling apart when key personnel leave. Your department heads no longer need to struggle with ways to keep their teams motivated to sell wellness and offer landmark experiences. Instead, they can focus on how to make things work more effectively to solve their guests' wellbeing problems.

3. It should bring structure, clarity and order

When a business is structured, clear and orderly, it gives your team confidence that they know what to do and how to do it, and it gives your guests confidence that your hotel knows what it is doing.

When it comes to your staff, the more structure, clarity and order you bring, the more likely you are to attract quality people who want to work with you and who want to deliver these landmark experiences. A good system gives them the tools they need to do outstanding work and to grow professionally. It also gives them the opportunity to learn how to do things properly.

When your suppliers see and perceive order, it gives them confidence that your business is a success, and they will want to be associated with your brand. No supplier wants to work with a brand that doesn't pay on time, is disorganised and does things on the fly, because that type of business rarely enjoys long-term success.

When it comes to your owners, your system gives them confidence in your ability to deliver the return on investment they are looking for. They recognise your ability to build a high-performance business that is not people-dependent, but systems-dependent – a business that is designed to grow successfully and adapt to changing market conditions.

Most importantly, you will have happy guests. They know they will get a consistently good experience each and every time they come, and they will happily recommend you and return.

HOW TO BUILD YOUR SYSTEM

Now that we are clear what we want your system to achieve, it's time to move on to how you can build such a system for your hotel.

There are three steps involved in creating the unique system that will differentiate you from your competitors:

1. Define all the elements you'll need to make your wellness concept work.
2. Identify where the possible problems in delivery may lie and take them into consideration.
3. Write the relevant processes and training plan.

1. Define all the elements you'll need to make your wellness concept work

In other words, how do you do wellness in your hotel? What makes your way so special? Without realising it, you already built the foundations of your system– your unique way of doing things– when you created your gyroscope in Expectation and devised the winning plan to solve your avatar's wellbeing problems and deliver the landmark experiences in Story. These are unique to your hotel.

In System, we take the winning plan you developed in Story along with the avatar's journey and brainstorm the essential elements you will need to make the concept work. We look at the entirety of your hotel: from how you sell and market it, take reservations, welcome your guests, keep facilities clean and in working order and provide the things you need to solve your avatar's wellbeing problems, to how you deliver the landmark experiences and keep your avatars engaged after their stay. How are they all involved in solving the wellness needs of your guest? What role does each of these elements play to help the end client get their prize?

Each and every element is key to ensuring you have a fully integrated wellness concept. Let's take the example from Story of the busy avatar with a stressful job suffering from family disharmony. Let's assume the winning plan is to allow them to make amends with their family and enjoy quality time together. To ensure we solve the problem of family disharmony, we will need to ensure that each family member's needs are met, not only those of the busy avatar. We will need to tailor the offer and target the marketing messages to adapt to each of their needs; we will need to gather all the relevant information for each family member and communicate that information to all the relevant people; we will need to create fun dining options that allow the family to spend quality time together (e.g., preparing a picnic basket or providing a cooking workshop where they can cook together); we will need to prepare activities that the family can do together (e.g., biking in the local area or making their own healing potions by mixing local herbs).

In System, you look at the entire journey of your avatar—from pre-arrival and arrival to post-departure – and carefully evaluate what you will need at each touchpoint to make sure their journey is as smooth as possible and your team have the tools they need to do their jobs properly.

At this stage, you don't need to worry about who will be doing what. You are looking at what needs to be done, irrespective of which department's job it is. We intentionally don't look at your system from a departmental point of view, to avoid compartmentalising your avatar's journey. When we look at our system in terms of the departments that make it up, we unwittingly fragment the guest experience because we make it about what falls within each department's scope of work instead of what the hotel (the guide) needs to solve the guest's wellbeing problems. If a small detail that adds value to the guest's experience (e.g., sending a follow-up message) falls out of the scope of work of one department, then that detail gets missed out and impacts the guest.

The questions you ask at this stage are: How can you build a wellness business that works predictably, effortlessly and profitably each and every day? How can you build a system that guarantees your avatar will get the landmark experience in exactly the same way every time? How do you build a wellness concept that will work without you, even long after you and your team have left? As Klaus Spierkermann highlighted in his interview in my *Wellness in Hospitality* series, it's important to think of those who will be taking over from you tomorrow. You can read the article here: **www.linkedin.com/pulse/wellness-hospitality-interview-klaus-spierkermann-sonal-uberoi.**

The idea here is to identify all the necessary elements you will need from start to finish – from the very beginning of the guest's journey to after they leave your hotel and beyond – to create the best system through which good wellness professionals can be leveraged to produce extraordinary results consistently.

EXERCISE 7
DEFINE YOUR UNIQUE ELEMENTS

Look at what makes your way so special. Each and every element is key to ensuring you have a fully integrated wellness concept.

Download the Special Way Canvas from the Wellness Business Essentials Toolkit at **www.spa-balance.com/wellness-business-essentials-toolkit/** and let's dive in:

1. Take your **Winning Plan Canvas** from Exercise 6 and your **Avatar's Journey Canvas** from Exercise 5 and brainstorm what elements you will need so that your team has the right tools to solve your avatar's wellbeing problems and deliver the landmark experiences. When I work with my clients, I encourage them to take a bird's eye view of their entire operation and then zero in to each touchpoint of their guest journey.

2. Once you've identified the key elements you'll need, think about what other tools you'd need if someone with no previous experience in the industry could pick the tool and deliver the landmark experiences. Remember the first golden rule of your system: it must be valuable and useful for all your stakeholders.

2. Identify where the possible problems in delivery may lie and take them into consideration

Once you have defined the different elements you will need to solve your avatar's wellbeing problems, and considered the tools someone with no previous experience would need to deliver your avatars the landmark experience, the next step is to make your system watertight. You do this by identifying where the possible problems in delivery of these landmark experiences could lie so you can pre-empt them and set your teams up for success.

We start by conducting an internal SWOT (Strengths, Weaknesses, Opportunities and Threats) analysis of the different elements of your hotel's operational machinery. Where do your strengths lie? What are the weakest links in the chain that may potentially cause problems later down the road? What external factors could throw a spanner in the works? Or what external factors could present a great opportunity for improving your system?

For example, your hotel might have acres and acres of land with gorgeous walking trails, but the big size of your grounds could make it challenging to service the different areas of the hotel. In this case, you would need to take into account the time it takes staff and guests to get from one area to another. A buggy service and clear signage would be essential elements, including the clustering of different leisure spaces so that guests do not need to go from one point of the hotel for their gym workout to another point for their yoga session.

You also need to consider temporary disruptions to your operations. We know it is impossible to plan for every adversity (as the pandemic showed us), but it is important to look at external factors that could negatively impact our ability to deliver the landmark experiences. For example, there might be a ground transportation project underway in your destination that will cause severe traffic jams and substantially increase the time it takes staff, guests and suppliers to get to your hotel. Eventually, though, the improved infrastructure will greatly reduce the time it takes for them to get to the hotel. You'd need to factor in the extra time in your system during the construction phase, as well as the impact on operations once the road is built.

These are just random examples, but this is the level of detail my clients start to look at in their operational system when I work with them. They understand the importance of being fully aware – or as aware as they can be at this stage of their project – of the potential problems that could affect the delivery of the landmark experiences their avatars are looking for before they pivot or implement their wellness offering.

TOP TIP 6

You create a watertight system by identifying the potential problems in delivery and pre-empting them by incorporating tools to help your teams avoid these problems.

Your system must be watertight. You achieve this by identifying the potential problems in delivery and pre-empting them by incorporating tools to help your teams avoid these problems. In the example of our busy avatar with a stressful job suffering from family disharmony, the potential problems in delivery of the family picnic could include poor weather conditions; in the case of a family cooking workshop, it could be a lack of space or staff, particularly in high season. In this case, the hotel would need to find and incorporate a workable solution into the system. For example, instead of relying on their fixed staff, they could collaborate with a local cook who will share their own tricks and recipes – and this could also be done at the cook's home to make the experience more authentic. A lack of space and staff could also be a problem for the family wellness activities, and the same solution of collaborating with a local guide could be incorporated into the system.

It is all too easy to say that you will figure it out along the way. However, unless you can pre-empt issues and come up with solutions, you will always be under-delivering and in a reactive mode. These are the types of problem that hinder the success of the wellness asset. Identifying these problems and thinking of the solutions at this early stage ensures you have a solid and efficient system in place, you get the right people on board and that when the concept is implemented, you and your team can confidently hit the ground running.

EXERCISE 8
KNOW YOUR BLIND SPOTS

Make your system watertight by identifying where the possible problems in delivery lie.

Open the Blind Spot SWOT Canvas from the Wellness Business Essentials Toolkit and let's dive in:

1. Carry out a SWOT analysis of your operational system to identify the weak links that could pose a problem in the delivery of the landmark experiences. Remember to consider factors that are external to your hotel but that could impact your operations.

2. Brainstorm the potential problems in delivery of the landmark experiences and incorporate checks into the system to pre-empt these problems. Remember these are problems that are external to your team's skills.

3. Write the relevant processes and training plan

Once you have identified the different elements that will be required for your team to consistently deliver outstanding results to your guests, you have brainstormed all the possible problems that could arise in the delivery of the landmark experiences, and you have created the solutions for them, the next step is to write the processes – for each and every element, you will need a process to deliver the landmark experiences consistently – and the plan for training your staff in them.

Traditionally, hoteliers have relied on detailed written standard operating procedures (SOPs), but in practice these are not always followed. The urgency of day-to-day operations means that new staff generally learn on the job from another staff member, in some cases rarely referring back to the SOP. When I work with my clients, I create a series of 'how-to' videos where the new member of staff can watch how things are done at their own pace and without taking up the time of another member of staff to train them. The how-to videos tend to be more effective for certain tasks, allowing staff to refer back to the video, pausing and playing as they perform the task. There are several affordable applications out there that can help you create on-brand how-to videos that are easy to edit.

To create a system that is efficient, effective and sustainable over the long run, your processes need to be simple, concise, repeatable and adaptable.

Simple

Your processes should be simple to implement, perform and tweak. They should be easy to understand and follow so that someone with no previous experience can pick them up and successfully perform the task. Simple processes make your staff's job of delivering the landmark experiences easier.

Concise

Your processes should be concise. Operations are high-pressure environments; your team does not have time to read pages and pages of SOPs to find out what they need to do. Your processes should be short and to the point, and should clearly indicate how each task should be performed.

Repeatable

Your processes should be repeatable. Your staff should be able to easily repeat tasks on a day-to-day basis, irrespective of the department they are in, their skill set or how long they have worked in the hotel. If your processes can't be repeated, they're too complicated or irrelevant.

Adaptable

Your processes should be adaptable. Rigid processes are equally as bad as no processes. Just as your avatar's needs evolve, so must your processes evolve to adapt to the changing market conditions. This does not mean they should be constantly changed, but they should be updated on a regular basis.

Hand-in-hand with your processes is the training plan for these processes. The factors you need to consider when creating your training plan are:

- How long will it realistically take a staff member to learn each process?

- Can the process be self-learned, or does the staff member need someone to train them? One thing we learned from the pandemic was the need to rapidly adapt to new realities and to streamline operations.

- Is there any specific order or priority to learn the processes?

- Which processes require on-site presence? Can some of them be learned remotely? Although the hospitality industry has traditionally required on-site presence for learning, there are processes that could be learned from home.

After this stage, you should have created 90% of your processes, as well as the training plan. As we are still in the blueprint phase (whether you have a current wellness offering that you want to change or you're looking to add a new one), around 10% of your system and processes will need to be added and tweaked at a later date once they've been up and running for a few months. We'll go over this process in Navigation and Consistency.

Writing processes can be mundane and time-consuming; when I work on projects, it is one of the important tasks I take on. For those hoteliers working on their wellness concept alone, I recommend you get an external specialist to write out the detailed processes, taking into account the potential problems in delivery. If you've never delivered this new wellness offering, then you may not be aware of a specific delivery problem that an expert would be able to flag easily. This expert must have a proven track record in writing processes for successful systems. As a hotelier, you will not have the time or the objectivity to write processes that are simple, concise, repeatable and adaptable. Where your contribution will be valuable is in looking at the strategic aspect of the system and processes.

EXERCISE 9
WRITE YOUR PROCESSES

Make your system efficient, effective and sustainable over the long run.

Open the Processes Canvas from the Wellness Business Essentials Toolkit and let's dive in:

1. Grab the **Special Way** Canvas from Exercise 7 as well as your **Blindspot SWOT Canvas** from Exercise 8 and write your processes for how your team can deliver your avatar their prize: the landmark experiences.

2. Once you've written your processes, write your training plan describing how your team will be trained on your special way of doing wellness.

At the end of these three steps, you will be able to clearly articulate how you do wellness at your hotel. You will have your own proprietary way of consistently delivering outstanding results. You will have created your system, a system that is unique to you.

CASE STUDIES

Let's take a look at the two case studies and see the System stage in action. Hotel Innovator followed the principles to create its own special way of doing wellness, while Hotel Traditionalist skipped the System stage and waited for its team to come on board and write the processes.

CASE STUDY

(WHEN THINGS ARE DONE RIGHT)

HOTEL INNOVATOR

The challenge

We created and stress-tested the wellness concept in Expectation, and in Story we aligned the Spa Sommelier concept with our avatar's wellness needs. The next step was to develop the right system for the hotel – their special way of doing wellness that guests would not find in any other hotel in the world.

The general manager was on a mission-based project: to make this hotel the best hotel in Iberia and to ensure it would consistently remain in this prized position. The challenge was to create a system that would be sustainable in the long run and that could be managed by a team with little experience and skill.

The approach

We began by brainstorming the key elements needed to build the best system for this hotel's reality. We knew from Story that time constraint was one of our avatar's villains, so our plan was to deliver a thoughtfully organised and orchestrated wellness experience during their stay that minimised the impact of their limited time.

We identified organisation and personalised, fuss-free service as the key elements of the wellness system. To achieve this level of service, we introduced the key figure of a personal butler, our avatar's personal assistant and their one-point contact with the rest of the hotel.

We exhaustively evaluated where the possible problems in delivery of these landmark experiences lay. We learned that check-in was a key time-waster for many of our guests; they didn't enjoy lining up and waiting to be checked in after a long trip. The other key obstacles were inaccurate or insufficient information about the likes and dislikes of each guest, the lack of fluid and effective communication within departments, and a rigid, overly engineered plan that didn't accommodate last-minute changes.

With the possible obstacles to delivery identified, we set out to create the processes, taking into consideration the best workable solutions. For example, to continue with the personalised service theme, once the guests arrived at the hotel (in the comfortable car with refreshments and free Wi-Fi access), they were taken straight to their room, where their butler did the check-in – which involved a quick passport scan and signing of the necessary paperwork – in two minutes. The guest could then settle in the comfort of their room. What made the arrival process so smooth was the fluid communication between departments. Concise, directed questions were added on to the Likes & Dislikes questionnaire (we went through several drafts before finalising the first working document) so that we got the necessary information to personalise each guest's experience before they arrived at the hotel.

We had clearly defined how wellness was done at the hotel so that we would be better positioned to find the right people to execute it.

The outcome

Even though the team were aware that this was not the definitive system (as guests' needs would evolve, so would the system and processes need to adapt to these changes), they now had a clearly defined way of doing things, of adding value to their stakeholders and of solving their guests' problems in a consistent way each and every time. The organised structure of the system gave the general manager confidence, assurance and clarity in the wellness offering, thereby strengthening the owning company's trust in his ability to successfully lead such a high-profile project.

Hotel Innovator's example shows that investing the necessary time and resources at this stage to write your hotel's unique system will save substantial time, costs and headaches in the long run. It brings clarity and structure earlier on in the process.

The traditional hoteliers get so caught up in the design stage that they miss the importance of carefully considering their proprietary system, their special way of doing things, at such an early phase in the project. They leave the system for a later stage when all their staff are on board. The end result is chaos, improvisation and insecurity with your staff, as we see in Hotel Traditionalist's case below.

CASE STUDY
(WHEN THINGS ARE DONE WRONG)

HOTEL TRADITIONALIST

The challenge

We saw in Expectation and Story that the hotel failed to create a reliable gyroscope and a winning plan for their avatar to get the prize. They didn't have a solid foundation upon which to build the structure of their wellness concept. There were three different directions to follow – the owners', the general manager's and the wellness guru's – and each stakeholder wanted their own direction to prevail.

The main challenge was trying to find one special way to do wellness at their hotel that took on board the different desires of all stakeholders and the constantly changing wellness offering.

The approach

None of the stakeholders had experience in opening such a facility, so they felt more comfortable following the traditional way of doing things – the way the hospitality industry had always followed. They left creating the system and processes for the team to do when they joined, so that they could own the SOPs by participating in the process.

Each manager wrote their own department's SOPs but, because they were running against tight deadlines, their top priority was to open their area on time. They were not thinking about how they would deliver their guests their landmark experience. Instead, they copied, pasted and adapted the SOPs of their previous hotel to this one. They only knew the traditional way of doing things in the hospitality industry, so they continued to do things the same way in this hotel. They were proud to have implemented the SOPs of a top brand in a small hotel; it assured them that they had benchmarked their standards of quality to those of the top brands.

The wellness department was no different. The system was a copy and paste of processes from world-renowned spas and the protocols and brand philosophy of their product house partners. But the processes didn't align with the hotel's SOPs or the reality of the hotel and what it was trying to achieve with its wellness offering; they only brought more confusion for the team as they tried to gather all the different protocols and combine them into one big manual for wellness.

For the owners and the general manager, it was not important to invest in expert help to design the right system. They opted for the traditional approach of hiring first, then creating the systems.

The outcome

The outcome was a lack of cohesion between departments. Each was doing their best to open on time, but no one really knew what they were doing or why they were doing it, hence the implementation process was based on guesswork and improvisation. As a result, things the team had not planned for kept popping up, which meant more items to be purchased, increasing costs further. Staff were desperate, given a task they weren't equipped to do, and the general manager was left with the typical feeling of overwhelm and not having things under control. He was frustrated and tired and the hotel was not yet open.

CONCLUSION

Your system is what will differentiate you from your competitors. What makes your hotel special is your unique, proprietary way of doing wellness, not the offering or facilities themselves. Hotels are complex bricks-and-mortar businesses, and wellness facilities only add to that complexity. Traditional hoteliers try to make their offering and facilities unique first, then unfairly make their teams think about how they will deliver those services. As a result, traditional hoteliers struggle because they manage in an ad hoc, haphazard way; their guests are unhappy because they have a different experience each day depending on which staff member they get; and their staff are confused and unsure about how to do their job.

The innovative and forward-thinking hoteliers focus on creating their special way of doing things because they understand that it is how they do things– how they make their guests happy– that matters, not their offering or facilities. They consider it their job to create a strong system that helps their staff do their job properly and successfully deliver the landmark experiences. As a result, they remove the unnecessary stress from operations, make their staff's lives easier and their guests' experience smoother, and save themselves money in the long run. Innovative and forward-thinking hoteliers have happier owners who are confident their concept won't fall apart when these dedicated general managers move on. These hoteliers manage from a place of wisdom, self-confidence and clarity.

KEY TAKE-HOMES

1. Your system is what differentiates you from the rest. It is your special way of doing things in your hotel.

2. Investing the time and effort in creating a robust system at the early planning stage will save you time, money and headaches in the long run.

3. A well-thought-out and carefully defined system brings clarity, structure and confidence to your staff. It frees them from having to reinvent the wheel and allows them to concentrate on what they like doing: delivering their guests the landmark experiences.

4. Your system ensures that your end client has a seamlessly perfect experience instead of a disjointed and fragmented one.

5. When you have a unique, proprietary way of doing things, it becomes easier to find the right talent, who want to do things the way you want them to. It also makes your life easier as you no longer need to be in fire-fighting mode.

CHAPTER 9
EXECUTION

I n System, we looked at defining how you do things in your hotel. Once the right system and processes are in place, the next step is to look at the team and talent you need to execute them. Finding staff with the right skill set, experience and attitude has always been a challenge in a highly competitive, people-centred market where there is always a risk that the staff you have trained will be poached by a competitor for a better salary, position or brand.

In this chapter, I'll walk you through the fourth stage of the model, Execution. In this stage, we look at pulling together the right people to deliver the landmark experiences according to your special way of doing wellness. We define who will do wellness in your hotel.

WHAT IS EXECUTION ABOUT?

Execution is about how to find, hire and retain the team you need to successfully implement and execute your wellness concept, without breaking budget. It is about organising and executing your wellness business in the most intelligent way possible. It is about putting together the right team that works in synergy and in harmony with one another to deliver the landmark experiences, without you needing to hire highly skilled, experienced or expensive talent that your profit and loss can't realistically sustain.

In this stage, you get your team aligned with your wellness concept and make it easy for them to do what you want them to do: deliver landmark experiences. It is in this stage that you see the benefits of all the groundwork you did in the previous stages of Expectation, Story and System.

In Execution, you create your lean and ideal team to do wellness in your hotel.

WHY IS EXECUTION IMPORTANT?

If it is the system, your proprietary way of doing things, that produces the results, it is your people who bring your system to life. Your people are your hotel's software. How your people interact with your guests impacts the guests' end experience and how they feel and talk about your brand. It is this one-on-one contact that determines how your guests feel in your hotel.

Execution is important because it:

- Defines the profile of the people you need to successfully implement your wellness concept

- Helps you find, hire and retain the right people to do wellness in your hotel without breaking budget

- Reinforces your special way of doing wellness in

your hotel that your avatar will not find elsewhere

- Prevents your business being subject to the whims of mood swings and lack of motivation

- Streamlines your headcount and organises your business in the most efficient and cost-effective way

- Allows you to deliver extraordinary results using ordinary people.

When you get Execution wrong, you organise your business around personalities instead of functions, responsibilities and accountability. You end up adapting job functions and roles according to the personality and skill set of each staff member. These constant changes lead to a lack of clarity as to what each person should do, what they're responsible for and to whom, and to what standards they're held. As a result, your operations don't run smoothly and you worry about finding experienced and skilled staff that might be over your budget.

HOW DO YOU GET EXECUTION RIGHT?

Getting your people right has been challenging even in the best of times, let alone in times of extreme crisis such as the ones we're living through now, where multitasking is essential for survival. The problem I've seen with my clients during this survival phase has been the crossover in functions between departments and roles. If everyone does everything, who is accountable for producing which result? Even if you have a clearly defined system in place, you still need to know who is doing what, who is responsible for what, who reports to whom, and how your staff members know they're doing things right (or wrong).

For any wellness concept to work, irrespective of its type, size or complexity, there are six main roles you need:

WELLNESS BUSINESS EXPERT

Scope of role

The Wellness Business Expert ensures wellness is carefully threaded into each stage of your avatar's wellness experience.

Importance of role

This role is important because it:

- Ensures the right team is in place and that each role is covered

- Builds and nurtures strong and fluid relationships between departments

- Saves you time, money and headache as you have expert input.

Skills needed

The skills needed for this role are:

- In-depth knowledge of wellness operations

- Strong business acumen and a customer-centric approach

- The ability to be 'in' as well as 'on' your wellness business.

Outcome of role

You have a solid and fully integrated wellness offering.

Works with

The Wellness Business Expert works closely with the hotel General Manager, the Director of Sales and Marketing, the Director of Finance and the Head of Operations.

Employment relationship

The expert can either be part of the payroll or a subcontractor.

HEAD OF OPERATIONS

Scope of role

The Head of Operations is on the ground and coordinates daily operations, liaises with staff and interacts with your guests.

Importance of role

This role is important because it:

- Reassures your team that they can turn to someone if they need help

- Inspires confidence in your guests that things are done well in your hotel

- Ensures that operations run smoothly.

Skills needed

The skills needed for this role are:

- The ability to effectively lead multi- and cross-disciplinary teams

- In-depth knowledge of wellness operations

- Business acumen.

Note: your Rooms Division Director or Hotel Manager are not the right profiles to take on this role.

Outcome of role

You have happy guests and happy staff, because operations flow smoothly.

Works with

This role works closely with the executive team and the General Manager.

Employment relationship

This role should ideally be taken on by someone on your payroll, as it requires being involved in daily operations.

WELLNESS TRAINER

Scope of role

The Wellness Trainer develops your team's wellness skills and coordinates the training of your entire team.

Importance of role

This role is important because it:

- Provides your team with the right knowledge and tools to do their job properly

- Guides your team on how to deliver landmark experiences

- Ensures consistency in standards of quality.

Skills needed

The skills needed for this specialist role are:

- Strong organisation and communications skills

- The ability to pull in the right professionals to provide training in each modality

- Demonstrable experience in teaching teams.

Note 1: your head therapist isn't always a good trainer.

Note 2: the Wellness Trainer does not have to, and cannot, be an expert at every wellness modality you offer.

Outcome of role

You have a knowledgeable and confident team. As a result, you have happier staff and guests.

Works with

This role works closely with Human Resources, the executive team, the Head of Operations and the Wellness Specialists.

Employment relationship

This role can either be external or internal, and is sometimes taken on by the Wellness Business Expert.

WELLNESS SPECIALISTS

Scope of role

Each Wellness Specialist works with specialists of other wellness modalities to solve your guests' wellbeing problems. For example, your physiotherapist works closely with your fitness specialist and nutritionist.

Importance of role

This role is important because it:

- Forms the backbone of your wellness offering

- Solves your guests' wellbeing problems through specialist therapy

- Ensures your guests are happy.

Skills needed

The skills needed for this role depend on the type of wellness offering you have and the specialisation required to deliver the landmark experiences, but they include:

- The necessary qualifications to practise the required wellness modality
- Experience of working in the hospitality industry.

Outcome of role

You have a robust and professional wellness offering that delivers the results it promises.

Works with

The Wellness Specialists work closely with the Wellness Business Expert, other Wellness Specialists, the Wellbeing Attendant and the Head of Operations.

Employment relationship

Your Wellness Specialists should be a mix of internal and external collaborators.

WELLBEING ATTENDANT

Scope of role

The Wellbeing Attendant has a dual role:

- They are the first point of contact with your guests, advising them of the different wellness options available.

- They provide a support function, liaising directly with the Wellness Specialists to ensure they have the necessary information for each guest.

Importance of role

This role is important because it:

- Ensures that your guests' wellness journey is smooth

- Ensures communication is fluid between specialists

- Ensures operations flow smoothly and that the facilities are in order.

Skills needed

The skills needed for this role are:

- Being people and service-oriented

- Being able to resolve customer problems effectively

- Having strong communication skills and the ability to liaise with different personality types.

Outcome of role

You have smoother operations and happier guests, and any guest complaints are dealt with in the moment.

Works with

This person works closely with the Wellness Specialists, the Head of Operations and other departments.

Employment relationship

A client-facing and daily operations role, the Wellbeing Attendant needs to be on your payroll.

BUSINESS OPTIMISATION EXPERT

Scope of role

The Business Optimisation Expert optimises your wellness business and ensures it's performing on target and according to the gyroscope you created in Expectation.

Importance of role

This role is important because it:

- Ensures you keep a close eye on your objectives

- Flags anomalies in performance

- Prevents your hotel from getting to the danger zone – the worst-case scenario.

Skills needed

The skills needed for this role are:

- Business savviness

- In-depth knowledge of the wellness business and of the relevant key performance indicators

- A diverse and proven track record of stellar business performance.

Outcome of role

You have an agile business that is reaching targets and successfully responding to changing market conditions.

Works with

The Business Optimisation Expert works closely with the General Manager and all heads of department.

Employment relationship

This role can be internal or external and can be taken on by the Wellness Business Expert.

You must be wondering 'Do I really need all these positions?' Well, the answer is: no. Note that I used the term 'roles' and not 'positions'. You don't need six different people, but you do need each of these roles. I'll explain later in the chapter.

Now that we know which roles you need to successfully implement and execute your wellness concept, I will walk you through how to incorporate these functions into your

— **“** —

HOTELS TEND TO ORGANISE THEIR

BUSINESS, PARTICULARLY THEIR

WELLNESS BUSINESS, AROUND

PERSONALITIES RATHER THAN

FUNCTIONS

— **”** —

hotel's operations in the most effective way, and within budget. The three main steps are:

1. Define your organisational chart, the roles needed and each of the positions in it.
2. Prototype each position's role in your organisational chart.
3. Create an environment that makes it possible for your people to do what you want them to do.

1. Define your organisational chart, the roles needed and each of the positions in it

As with most people-centred industries, hotels tend to organise their business, particularly their wellness business, around personalities rather than functions. They organise their business around people rather than accountabilities or responsibilities, even if they have an organisational chart. Hence, when key talent leaves, part of their business goes with them and the cycle repeats with the next general manager or wellness director.

Hoteliers write their organisational charts based on the traditional positions in the industry: general manager and, reporting to them, the hotel manager and their executive team (director of finance, director of sales and marketing, director of food and beverage, director of rooms, and depending on the size of the wellness operation and hotel, director of wellness). They then define the role of each position according to the person who occupies it.

In Execution, we write your hotel's organisational chart according to your system – your special way of doing things – rather than the norms of the hospitality industry. We take your proprietary way of doing things and define the roles you will need to execute the winning plan you created in Story to solve your guests' wellbeing problems and deliver them the landmark experiences.

Each role takes on a number of functions and tasks, so we take all the functions you listed in System and group them into specific roles; for example, all the functions related to communicating with the guest before they arrive could be grouped into the role of Guest Relations. We do this for all the functions along your avatar's journey.

Before we delve further, I'd like to emphasise the difference between roles and positions. The position relates to where a particular person is placed within your organisational chart, who they report to and what they're accountable for. The role is the functions and responsibilities assumed by a particular position. Each position within the organisational chart can assume more than one role; for example, you might have someone in the position of Wellness Director in your organisational chart who takes on the roles of Head of Operations, Wellness Business Expert and Performance Booster Expert. Keeping in mind the difference between position and role helps you to create an efficient and streamlined organisational chart.

TOP TIP 7

Structure your organisational chart according to functions, roles and responsibilities instead of specific positions.

With this difference in mind, we consider the following key points:

- **What is my staffing budget for wellness?** If you don't have a set budget put aside, then allocate a specific amount for wellness staff. If you do have a set budget, although it's a good starting point, look beyond what you've always done. For example, if staffing costs have always been 40% of total wellness revenue, it doesn't necessarily mean that is the budget you need; it could be more or it could be less. However, it is important to identify your maximum figure.

- **What positions can my profit and loss realistically sustain?** Look at your hotel's overall profit and loss, not just departmental ones. Individual departmental profits and losses can be misleading because some departments are more labour-intensive than others; however, their indirect contribution to your overall top and bottom line can be significant. Cutting back on staff in these areas will negatively impact your overall profit and loss.

- **What is a competitive salary package for each position?** Research what the going market rates are for each of the positions you have in mind. Create a salary and benefits matrix that clearly marks the different salary brackets and benefits packages against the skills and experience level the staff member should have. Be fair in your approach and, where possible, align packages according to the responsibility and impact of the role on your top and bottom line as well as guest satisfaction.

- **Where does each position fit within my hotel's big picture?** Who reports to whom? What are their responsibilities? What are they accountable for? What impact does each position have on the overall business? We sometimes fall into the trap of doing things the way they have always been done, even though that way may no longer make sense in today's reality. Each position on your organisational chart should be an integral part of your big-picture objectives.

Detail each of the positions, from the top down, and indicate the results to be achieved by each one. At this point you are concentrating on your hotel operations and what is needed. For example, it might be a mid-scale urban hotel with 100 rooms that predominantly caters to corporate clients and is looking to add a small wellness offering. For its operations to work, it needs the following main positions: reporting to the general manager are the director of sales and marketing, director of finance, director of food and beverage, and the director of rooms. The hotel probably does not have the budget for a wellness manager, so it allocates that role to a senior wellness professional. Its organisational chart could look something like this:

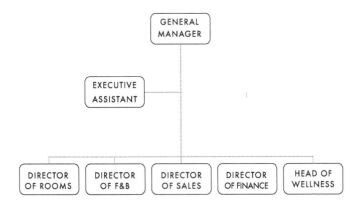

The next step is to take the six essential roles needed to implement your wellness concept and add them to the positions in your organisational chart. For example, if your current or projected direct revenue from your wellness offering is less than €250,000 a year, your hotel will struggle to sustain the cost of six different people to take on these key roles. In this case, the key positions could be:

- Wellness Business Expert (not necessarily part of your payroll)

- Wellness Specialists (some can be on your payroll, others freelancers)

- Wellbeing Attendants (on your payroll).

For the remaining three roles – Head of Operations, Trainer and Business Optimisation Expert – you carefully identify which of the positions listed above will take on these additional roles.

Referring back to the mid-scale urban hotel, the Wellness Business Expert could be a freelance consultant who takes on the roles of Head of Operations, Trainer and Business Optimisation Expert.

We have seen that, although your hotel might not have the budget to hire six different positions, they can still ensure that these essential roles are covered by other positions.

EXERCISE 10

WRITE YOUR ORGANISATIONAL CHART

Structure your organisational chart according to functions, roles and responsibilities instead of specific positions.

Download the **Lean & Ideal Team Canvas** from the Wellness Business Essentials Toolkit at **www.spa-balance. com/wellness-business-essentials-toolkit/**, click on the tab 'Organisational Chart' and let's dive in:

1. Grab your **Special Way Canvas** from Exercise 7 and the **Processes Canvas** from Exercise 9 and carefully define the functions and roles you'll need to do wellness in your hotel.

2. Refer back to your **Wellness Concept Value Canvas** from Exercise 1, particularly the How section (the best, ideal and worst-case scenarios). Based on those numbers, draft your organisational chart.

2. Prototype each position's roles in your organisational chart

Now that you know the positions your hotel needs to fill to deliver the landmark experiences, and the roles and functions each position will carry out, the next step is to indicate what results are to be achieved by each role within each position, what the position will be accountable for, and a list of standards by which the results will be evaluated.

TOP TIP 8

Prototype every role so you can draw a detailed picture of what each role 'looks' like: what functions it takes on, what results are expected from each role, what it will be accountable for and to whom.

This exercise is called prototyping. We are essentially creating a 'prototype' of every role in each of the positions in your organisational chart. In other words, we are drawing a detailed picture of what each role 'looks' like.

Prototyping each role is important because:

- **It brings clarity to each role** by considering what each role does, how they do it, what results are expected of each role, what each role is accountable for and to what standards each role will be held accountable.

- **It prevents you from changing your job descriptions** to match the skill set of either a person you're tempted to pass a certain role on to – someone you like and work well with – or someone 'imposed' on you who might not have the required essential skill set to take that role on.

- **It makes your operations more responsive** to market shifts. For example, in light of hiring a lot of new staff in a short space of time (e.g., in high season) or suddenly having to downsize your team (e.g., in an economic downturn).

It is important to understand that we prototype each role, but not each position. To reiterate: a role is what your team member does, whereas a position is where the team member sits within your organisational chart.

One lesson we learned from the crisis brought on by the 2020 pandemic was the need to multitask. When hotels were able to reopen their doors with a greatly reduced occupancy, the positions that were retained were required to take on several roles, to wear different hats and to do these jobs to the best of their abilities; they had no choice. Many hotels suddenly found themselves rewriting job descriptions or going off-script to survive and get things done. Many staff members had to be retrained for their 'new' jobs because job descriptions were written according to the position each person held in the hotel (director of sales and marketing, director of spa etc.) instead of being written according to the roles each position was responsible for (actively promoting the hotel, overseeing the wellness operation etc.).

If we had prototyped each and every role needed in our system to give the winning plan to the avatar, then we wouldn't have needed to rewrite job descriptions, roles and accountabilities when we had to eliminate certain positions. Instead, we could have rearranged the roles under the new positions on the updated organisational chart.

If you scored low on Execution in the ESSENCE scorecard, take your time working on the roles needed to do wellness properly in your hotel.

To prototype each role, you need to pull out the avatar journey we mapped out in Story along with the winning plan. You'll also need the processes we wrote in System. With these key tools at hand, ask yourself the following questions for each role:

- What functions will this role cover within the system?

- How will this role help to solve my avatar's problems and deliver their prize?

- Is this role essential, or a 'nice to have'?

- How could I make this role as effective as possible while also maximising profits?

- How could I give the person responsible for this role the best possible experience? For example, due to streamlining of operations the fitness trainer is required to clean down and disinfect the gym at the end of their shift. Keeping the gym clean and safe for both your guests and your staff is important, but the exhaustive measures can get mundane and draining after a while. To keep your qualified fitness instructor – who studied hard to train guests, not to dedicate an important chunk of their time to cleaning – motivated, you could introduce a points system to give them rewards in the hotel's restaurant or spa.

When you are clear what functions each role will have, what it will be accountable for, by what standards it will be evaluated and which position in the organisational chart will be responsible for the role, it makes it easier for you to find the staff you need to deliver the landmark experiences.

While it is only natural to want to find the most skilled and experienced wellness professionals, what you are actually looking for are professionals who are willing to learn and grow: people who care about doing it right, people for whom questions haven't become answers. These people could very well already be on your payroll; perhaps they could take on these roles if they were given the right training and tools.

I'm not saying that skill, expertise and experience aren't important. They are very important. However, attitude is even more important. You aren't hiring for skill, but for the ability to perform the necessary functions of the corresponding roles and to deliver the prize for your guests in your hotel's unique way, not your staff member's way or what they think is the best way. Your talent's valuable input is in their creativity and the quality of the job done, not in changing protocols according to the way they are used to doing things.

Once we have found and hired the people who will be carrying out each of the roles according to the organisational chart and the prototype, the next step is about how we get our people to do what we want them to and in the way we want them to do it.

EXERCISE 11
PROTOTYPE YOUR ROLES

Paint a picture of what each role will 'look' like for the person who will be responsible for that role.

Open the **Lean & Ideal Team Canvas** from Exercise 10, click on the tab 'Prototype' and let's dive in:

1. With your team, look at the functions each role will cover. You'll need to refer back to the list of functions and roles you created for your organisational chart in Exercise 10, the **Avatar's Journey Canvas** from Exercise 5, the **Winning Plan Canvas** from Exercise 6 and the **Processes Canvas** from Exercise 9.

2. Narrow down the roles to the most essential ones and allocate the relevant roles to each position in your Organisational Chart from Exercise 10.

3. Create an environment that makes it possible for your people to do what you want them to do

In the previous steps, we organised your business in the most intelligent way possible. We identified the most important positions, what results were expected of them, what they were accountable for and the standards to which they would be evaluated. We also prototyped every role each position would assume, to ensure each one of them helps your avatar get their prize in the best and the most profitable way, while making it easy, fun and fulfilling for the person that would take on that role. We now work on how you can make your staff follow your plan, consistently and fulfillingly.

To get your people to do what you want them to do, you need to create an environment that makes it natural and possible for them. It's your job to create an environment that makes it easy, fun and fulfilling for staff to perform their roles and responsibilities. If you want your hotel to deliver wellness properly, you need to create an environment that is conducive to wellbeing– an environment that is well.

You create such an environment by having the right leadership, culture and reward.

Leadership

The right leadership does not need to be comprised of the most experienced, skilled or highly paid people. It does not mean you promote your most capable therapist to wellness manager without the proper training, or that you leave your wellness offering without an appropriate leader and make the spa supervisor take on responsibilities that are above their pay or skill level. It means you find people who believe in the system you have created, your proprietary way of doing things, and provide them with the necessary tools and training to do their job properly. Their central focus should be on helping their teams to deliver the landmark experiences by following the way your hotel does wellness.

Your leaders should be processes and results driven. Their job is to make sure that the system is being executed as well as it can be and that the results are being delivered. Each leader's role is to guide their team through the processes so that they can, in turn, guide the guests through their wellness journey to the prize.

Culture

The right culture comprises the values, practices and objectives that put the wellbeing of your guests and team front and centre. You know you have the right culture when the culture you describe to your stakeholders is the same as the actual culture in your hotel (the way your people really act and how they treat one another).

The tradition in the hospitality industry has always been one of gruelling work conditions with changing shifts, long hours, working during weekends and public holidays and, in some cases, working several days on end and having days off removed at the last minute. As we saw from Harsh Truth 6 in Chapter 4, your guests' wellbeing can only be achieved through your staff's wellbeing.

While we can't plan for every eventuality or pre-empt every mishap in daily operations, we can ensure our teams have some sort of work–life balance and that their wellness is taken into consideration. A team that is well is more likely to deliver your guests their landmark experiences than a team that is overworked, tired or burnt out.

Reward

The right reward comes in the form of recognition and growth. When your team feels rewarded, it is happier, and so are your guests.

The innovative and forward-thinking hoteliers recognise the good work and value of their teams. Their teams feel appreciated and, as a result, they are more productive, motivated and inspired to improve their work and deliver landmark experiences each and every time. They embed recognition throughout their operations via verbal acknowledgements, written letters and other accolades. They openly express their gratitude for their team's work.

Growth is an integral part of team satisfaction. As emotional beings, we're driven by progress and growth. We want to feel a sense of achievement. The innovative and forward-thinking hoteliers provide their teams with real growth opportunities. They take a real interest in developing their teams and guiding them through their personal and professional progression. As a result, their teams enjoy greater job satisfaction, perform better and are more committed to the hotel's special way of doing wellness.

EXERCISE 12
CREATE A 'WELL' ENVIRONMENT

You can't offer wellness if you don't have an environment that is 'well' for your team.

Open the **Lean & Ideal Team Canvas** from Exercise 10, click on the tab 'Well Environment' and let's dive in:

1. Write your internal Wellness Manifesto and train your leaders on how to become the guide of their teams.

2. Instil a 'well' culture and ensure the Wellness Manifesto is practised in day-to-day operations.

Together with your heads of department, create a reward programme that incorporates recognition and growth prospects.

CASE STUDIES

Let's take a look at the two case studies and see the Execution stage in action. Hotel Innovator followed the principles in Execution and, without hiring highly skilled or expensive staff, put together a lean and ideal team that successfully delivered landmark experiences. Hotel Traditionalist hired highly skilled and experienced staff, but it could barely afford to show them how to do things. This team changed things without success, eventually leaving and costing the hotel thousands of dollars by developing ideas that didn't work.

CASE STUDY

(WHEN THINGS ARE DONE RIGHT)

HOTEL INNOVATOR

The challenge

The hotel was small and in a location where the local talent had limited knowledge of wellness and little experience of working in a luxury environment. Additionally, as our avatar was predominantly international, we needed staff who spoke a second language, which further reduced the available talent pool. The challenge was in finding the right people who aligned with our brand values and who were willing to do things the way we did in our hotel, but without breaking budget.

The approach

We started by revisiting the hotel's organisational chart, which had been drafted before the owners had planned to make wellness one of their core drivers.

We took the journey we mapped out in Story, and our unique way of delivering the landmark experiences to our guests from System, and identified the key roles that would be needed. From there, we identified the key positions we'd need, taking into account the budget we had created in Expectation. We did this by looking at their functions and accountability instead of their ideal skill and experience. This prevented the general manager from planning the staffing requirements based on colleagues he had worked with in a previous hotel and his belief that it would be wonderful to have them here and repeat the success story.

We evaluated all the roles needed to execute the winning plan. Our focus was to be the best guides, journeying together with our avatar to the end prize (the landmark experiences), so we defined the roles in a more holistic way, instead of hospitality's traditional way of splitting them according to departments. Our central question was: what roles are needed at which stage of the journey?

We prototyped each of the clearly defined roles. We stepped into the shoes of the team member who would take on this role and asked ourselves what exactly they would need. What were their objectives? How were they going to carry out the role? What would they be accountable for, to whom, and to what standards? And how would they know whether they were doing it right?

After prototyping each role, we allocated it to the relevant position in the organisational chart.

The outcome

The tide had turned for the general manager. The success of his wellness offering no longer depended on the experience and skill of his people. He no longer stressed about finding experienced, skilled talent prepared to work in such a remote location. Instead, he had local talent with great potential lining up to be part of his team because they wanted to do something different and meaningful. The hotel successfully delivered landmark experiences without breaking budget. As a result, the owning company fully trusted his leadership abilities.

CASE STUDY
(WHEN THINGS ARE DONE WRONG)

HOTEL TRADITIONALIST

The challenge

The hotel suffered a snowball effect of problems being added on to the problems from the previous stages. The lack of a coherent budget from Expectation made it difficult to know what headcount they could sustain. From Story, the lack of a clear wellness offering meant things changed constantly, and from System the inexperienced wellness guru and team were left with the task of writing protocols with no previous experience. The main challenge in Execution was to find, hire and train the right people who were willing and prepared to deliver the different prizes each stakeholder had in mind, while keeping manning costs to a minimum.

The approach

The lack of a clearly defined budget meant the team weren't fully aware of when they were crossing budget. Additionally, because of all the last-minute expenses that hadn't been accounted for, the pressure was on to keep the ever-increasing costs to an absolute bare minimum. Only essential staff could be hired to cover shifts (not taking into account sick leave, public holidays and vacations).

This was a family-owned and run hotel with an informal organisational chart. They created positions and hired staff by focusing on the skill and experience they believed they needed or thought nice to have, which was essentially the skill and experience they felt they lacked. The subjective criteria for hiring staff meant that in some cases they went beyond the marked salary range for a position to meet the demands of the candidate they wanted, even if they knew they were over-paying.

The remaining positions were covered under the pressure of working against the clock to open doors by the scheduled date. The team were forced to hire people who were willing and able to work with them at such short notice, but who perhaps didn't have the right profile to execute the wellness concept.

The staff who were hired hit the ground running, with everyone all-hands-on-deck and jumping in wherever needed, but without the right tools or the knowledge of what exactly they were supposed to do and how. No one was responsible or accountable for any specific task. Training was cut short so that staff could fill in on more urgent tasks. Training, they thought, could be given once operations launched.

The outcome

The owners successfully opened the hotel on the scheduled date; however, this came with a hefty price tag. The disparity in salary figures between staff led to tension, resentment and friction, as some team members felt they were treated unfairly. The staff were overworked, tired and confused as to what their job was. They had come with the intention of wanting to learn something new, in giving their best to their guests and in contributing to the goal of sustainable wellness– but what they found was chaos and lack of direction. The entire pre-opening team left within a few weeks of opening, making the already exhausted general manager's life even harder and costing the hotel more in replacing them.

CONCLUSION

If it is the one-on-one contact your people have with your guests that determines how your guests feel in your hotel, then it is vital to consider how easy you make it for your people to do their job. The traditional hoteliers plan their business around the skill, expertise and experience of their people. They believe that, because they have hired skilled talent, their people already know what to do and how to do it; they don't need guidance. They let their skilled talent lead the way in their respective areas, and as a result, they become dependent on that specific talent. They enjoy the energy and passion of experienced and skilled talent at the beginning, but later struggle to keep this talent motivated with the right growth opportunities. Eventually, they lose them to a better brand or a higher salary. Then they repeat this vicious cycle.

Innovative and forward-thinking hoteliers understand that they do not need extraordinary people to deliver landmark experiences. They opt for ordinary but keen people who are capable of producing extraordinary results, rather than hiring talent they cannot afford and breaking their budget. Innovative and forward-thinking hoteliers have teams that want to do things the way their hotel wants them to be done, because they have guidance and structure. They have teams that are happier, more motivated and more engaged, and clients who enjoy the landmark experiences they are looking for. As a result, they save the costs of constantly hiring and training staff. They make their lives a lot easier, freeing themselves from fire-fighting. Instead, they do the thing they like and want to do: manage the hotel in a strategic rather than a reactive way.

KEY TAKE-HOMES

1. You don't need the most experienced, skilled or expert team to deliver the landmark experiences; you need an ordinary yet winning team that is willing to do extraordinary things.

2. The 'position' relates to where a particular person is placed within your organisational chart, who they report to and what they're accountable for.

3. The 'role' is the functions and responsibilities assumed by a particular position.

4. Write your organisational chart based on your budget and the roles each of the positions will take on.

5. Prototype each of the roles you'll need to deliver your guests the landmark experiences.

6. Innovative and forward-thinking hoteliers organise their businesses around functions and accountability instead of personalities and skill set. They successfully deliver landmark experiences without breaking budget.

CHAPTER 10
NAVIGATION

In the first two stages, Expectation and Story, we worked on creating the best wellness concept for your hotel, one that considers what you as a hotelier want to offer and also what your clients want to experience. In System and Execution, we worked on implementing your wellness concept in the most effective way for your guests and your staff. We worked on creating your special way of doing wellness and we found, hired, trained and retained the ordinary people who deliver extraordinary results without breaking our budget.

The next stages– Navigation and Consistency– ensure you are aligned with your big-picture goal and continue to deliver the landmark experiences consistently.

WHAT IS NAVIGATION ABOUT?

Navigation is about course correction. It is about nudging your operations back on track. Even when we have the right systems and people in place, the daily grind of operations tends to throw us off course. I've seen this happen even in the most organised of settings. In this stage, we turn to your business's gyroscope – the one we created in Expectation – to steer your concept back on track. We work on the small and seemingly insignificant actions that are easy to do (and also easy not to do) but will make a big difference in keeping your big-picture goal – to create and deliver landmark experiences – in mind. Navigation is about remaining aligned and keeping your ear to the ground.

In Navigation, we make strategic iteration part of your special way of doing things.

WHY IS NAVIGATION IMPORTANT?

Just as there is never a perfect day to open doors when it comes to new builds, there is never a perfect operation, even in well-established brands. Your entire operation is a constant work in progress – and that includes your wellness offering.

Navigation is important because it:

- Ensures that your operations are constantly aligned with your big-picture goals

- Keeps your team focused on why they are doing things: to solve your avatar's wellbeing problems and get them to their prize

- Prevents you from going off course and being led astray by the next trending therapy, shiny piece of equipment or wellness guru

- Encourages you and your team to keep close to your avatars and listen to their real wellbeing problems

- Saves you money because it prevents you from hastily jumping into Band-Aid solutions that don't work

- Ensures you regularly fine-tune your offering to keep it current and relevant.

When you get Navigation wrong, you get easily sidetracked by market trends and distracted by well-intentioned but unhelpful feedback from different sources (even reliable sources). As a result, you unwittingly throw your team and yourself off track and you end up losing sight of your big-picture goals. You get into the danger zone of potentially making costly mistakes that aren't always easy to correct later down the line.

HOW DO YOU GET NAVIGATION RIGHT?

It is said that the Apollo rocket was on course to the moon for only 3% of the time. It was a highly sophisticated and finely calibrated work of engineering, with the world's best scientists helping it on its way, yet it was off course 97% of the time. For 29 minutes out of every 30, it was correcting its own navigation errors.

Even the finest pieces of machinery need calibrating to continue functioning optimally, and your hotel's operations machinery is no exception. No matter how strong your team, how solid your operating system, or how superlative your wellness offering, the reality is that your business will be off

"

NO MATTER HOW STRONG
YOUR TEAM, HOW SOLID YOUR
OPERATING SYSTEM, OR HOW
SUPERLATIVE YOUR WELLNESS
OFFERING, THE REALITY IS THAT
YOUR BUSINESS WILL BE OFF
COURSE FOR THE MAJORITY OF
THE TIME

"

course for the majority of the time. You will spend most of your time nudging it back onto the right path.

You will also need to continuously fine-tune your offering to keep it relevant and aligned with your gyroscope and your avatar's wellbeing needs. You will need to constantly tweak and improve your offering to ensure you are effectively solving your guests' wellbeing problems.

The reason you need to keep adjusting your offering and nudging your operations back on track is not that your system is faulty, your wellness concept doesn't work or your team isn't good. You need to constantly nudge your operations back on track because of the consistent series of tiny, seemingly insignificant actions that are easy to do (because they are part of your processes and daily operations), but at the same time easy *not* to do (because each one seems so insignificant that not doing it one day won't really affect your operations). This happens to all businesses.

For example:

We know all new staff must try a wellness-related service as soon as they're on board. However, in peak season (and particularly in these unprecedented times) it's easy to skip this part during the induction training and postpone it until things are quieter.

We know how important it is for our staff to be thoroughly trained on our system and processes. However, when you're short of staff and the new employee is experienced, it's tempting to skip the training and fast-track the onboarding process.

We know our therapists need to be trained on all treatments (provided they have the right qualifications), but it's easy to fold under the pressure of revenue targets and take on the extra last-minute booking instead of making time for training in a not very popular treatment.

These are examples of the small, seemingly insignificant actions that keep your operations and offering on track. They are strategic and critical, and when you do them consistently over time, their positive impact is compounded. However, if you skip them once or twice, they don't have a noticeable impact on your avatar's landmark experience or your hotel's operations.

Generally, the results of this series of small, seemingly insignificant actions aren't truly appreciated until a few months after you stop doing them. As the results aren't visible straightaway, these slow-burner activities that require discipline, commitment and constancy soon become unappealing, repetitive and mindless for the team to do. This is why many businesses (not only hotels) don't stick with these actions despite knowing they're important.

These activities grow unappealing, repetitive and mindless for the following reasons:

1. Training that appears ad hoc, ineffective and not useful

A vast majority of the problems in operations that cause us to go off track are related to problems in training. Problems occur either because we have dropped the ball when it comes to training our teams, or because our teams aren't engaged in the training we provide. We approach their training in the wrong way, making it appear irrelevant either to their day-to-day activities or their long-term career goals.

Examples include:

- **Lack of budget.** Human Resources and other department heads have to compromise their great ideas for training and use cheaper, less relevant alternatives.

- **One-size-fits-all approach to training.** When we standardise training, we assume that all staff want to learn the same things or that they all learn in the same way and require the same number of hours of training.

- **Misconceived ideas around training.** We approach training as something we must do to maintain standards and something our staff should be grateful for, rather than thinking about the purpose of the training in the first place.

- **Inconvenient training schedules.** Operations can be unpredictable, and it is inevitable that some training sessions will occur during an employee's personal time. After gruelling hours in operations, staff understandably prefer to rest during their time off instead of attending training.

- **Real attendance.** The reality is that not all staff members have the opportunity to attend the training sessions; they are pulled into operations when someone is ill, on holiday, on their day off or on a different shift.

2. Rigid systems

In System, we learned that strong systems are clearly defined, robust and flexible. They respond to shifting market conditions and evolving operations. Systems that are rigid and don't allow for flexibility eventually make tasks unappealing, repetitive and mindless.

Examples include:

- A meal option that cannot have an ingredient added or removed (in response to guest preference rather than an allergy)

- Strict treatment protocols that do not allow the therapist to adapt the massage according to the guest's needs

- Forcing a sale after a treatment when the guest prefers to enjoy their relaxation time and buy later, perhaps when they're back home

- Refusing a guest another towel because the policy is one towel per guest (supposedly due to environmental reasons, although the main reason is cost-cutting)

- Giving guests only one small water bottle each day, when most guests usually consume a litre of water a day during their stay.

This rigid approach makes tasks seem pointless, and eventually your team stops doing them. However, these actions could actually be a very important part of the system. For example, if we adapted each dish to every guest's preferences, it would not be very practical and ultimately it would affect the quality of landmark experiences. But the reason your team stopped doing these actions was because the system wasn't tweaked to take into account customer and staff feedback.

I will explain later in this chapter how you can avoid making your systems too rigid.

3. Loss of perceived value

It is easy to lose sight of why we do certain activities as we get absorbed by the daily grind of operations. We get caught up in the routine of doing things, without remembering why we do them and what value they add to us or the end client. We focus on the small, day-to-day activities, the minuscule detail that is perhaps urgent but not important, and we lose sight of the big picture.

Examples of such actions include:

- Performing the foot bath ritual before every treatment; it is easy to skip this, particularly when therapists have back-to-back treatments and are short of time

- Spending five minutes with your guest to go over their wellbeing concerns, giving tips to help them or booking them in for another treatment

- Giving the guest an extra minute or two of massage so they feel special and spoiled

- Allowing the guest to rest in the treatment room for five minutes after the treatment, instead of rushing them out because you have another client waiting

- Daily stocktake of treatment rooms to ensure products and linen are replenished, instead of discovering something is missing when in the room with the guest and having to pop out for it mid-treatment.

For your team, these small and seemingly insignificant actions might not seem as important as delivering the treatment or service, but these are precisely the details that, if missed, compromise the quality of our guests' landmark experiences and negatively impact brand image and business in the long run.

We have seen why you need to continuously fine-tune your offering to take into account valuable guest and staff feedback. We have also seen how these easy-to-do, and at the same time easy-not-to-do, actions become easier to neglect over the course of time and why they're important.

STAYING ON TRACK

I'll now show you how to fine-tune your offering effectively and steer your operations back on track. I'll show you how to use guest and staff feedback to calibrate your offering and how to make these small, seemingly insignificant points become actions that are viewed by your team as critical, strategic and meaningful. You will need your hotel's gyroscope that you created in Expectation.

1. Create an environment of intentional learning

We provide our staff with training so they can learn how we do things at our hotel. When we create an environment that stimulates the learning process, we shift our mindset from force-feeding too much or irrelevant information to that of fostering a nurturing environment centred around intentional learning.

Intentional learning is learning that is motivated by intentions and is goal directed. This means that when our teams (the learners) engage in intentional learning, they actively participate in their learning process. They take ownership of their learning and growth process.

Intentional learning is important because it makes us look at the training we provide from our team's point of view: what kind of information is useful for them, what stimulates them, what makes them grow professionally, what makes it easier and more fun for them to do their work, what complementary training will encourage lateral thinking, and so on.

When you have the culture of intentional learning embedded in your business, it ensures that:

- The small, seemingly insignificant and potentially mundane talent development actions are carried out because they have an important purpose that both you and your team are aware of

- You can clearly distinguish the glitches in your offering or system from the glitches caused by your team as part of their learning process.

You do this by implementing the following talent development actions.

Pre-start 'getting-to-know-you' sessions

Create a pre-start 'getting-to-know-you' session script that all your department heads follow, with specific questions aimed at knowing the new employee's goals, their growth aspirations, and their likes and dislikes. These sessions must take place before the new employee starts. Their purpose is two-fold: first, they allow us to get to know our new employee and vice versa (the new employee gets to know their manager and the company before they start); and second, they ensure both the manager and the employee actively participate in their individual and collective growth plan.

Tailored onboarding plans

With the valuable information you obtain from the 'getting-to-know-you' session, create a tailored onboarding plan for the new employee. Each person is unique, and so is the way they learn. A one-size-fits-all approach to onboarding might seem quicker and more practical; however, in the long run, it is more time-consuming and costly. The more time and patience you invest in getting each employee up to speed in the beginning, the less time and money you will spend in correcting their mistakes and managing them later down the road.

Targeted refresher training

After successfully onboarding each new member, create targeted refresher training plans that take into account each individual's learning needs and long-term career growth objectives. Some team members may need several refresher training sessions to get up to scratch, while others might only need a couple. When you focus the refresher training towards aligning each of your team members with the gyroscope and the winning plan to solve guests' wellbeing problems and deliver landmark experiences, you make it useful, engaging and fun, instead of mundane, disengaging and boring.

Standardised exit interviews

Standardised exit interviews are a valuable source of information. They give you the opportunity to learn from your staff what went wrong and what they enjoyed. Our unhappiest staff members are sometimes our greatest teachers. They give insight into a different perspective that many times we don't consider because we're busy keeping our star performers happy. Write out a script with targeted questions about areas you can improve. To get open and constructive feedback, a manager who was not the direct supervisor of the employee should conduct the interview.

Regular 'how-are-you-getting-along?' chats

The regular 'how-are-you-getting-along?' chats are different from performance appraisals. These chats don't measure employee performance, but instead seek to understand how each of your team members is getting along and whether there is anything you can do to make their experience more enjoyable. You can't successfully offer wellness if you do not create an environment that is well for your team – the guides who journey together with your avatar towards their prize. These regular chats help nudge you and your entire team back on course and keep them aligned to your gyroscope.

TOP TIP 9

Just as your client's journey does not start and end at your hotel, neither does the journey of your team members with you. The pre-commencement and post-completion phases are great opportunities to intentionally learn and grow.

When you implement the above five talent development actions, you systematically ensure you have an environment that fosters intentional learning. Both your hotel and your staff open up to learning to do things better– to executing the winning plan and solving your guests' wellbeing problems better.

EXERCISE 13
INCORPORATE INTENTIONAL LEARNING

Create an environment that stimulates your team's learning process.

Download the **Course Correction Canvas** from the Wellness Business Essentials Toolkit at **www.spa-balance.com/wellness-business-essentials-toolkit/**, click on the tab 'Intentional Learning' and let's dive in:

1. Together with your department heads and human resources team, brainstorm what questions you

would like to add to the pre-start 'getting-to-know-you' sessions and the standardised exit interviews. Refer back to your **Gyroscope Canvas** from Exercise 3 in Expectation and the **Winning Plan Canvas** from Exercise 6 in Story and think about what information will be useful to ensure you are consistently delivering landmark experiences.

2. Together with your human resources team, draft an onboarding and refresher training plan for your department heads to use for their teams. The aim is to get all staff to the same end destination: everyone executing your special way of doing wellness in the same way to deliver landmark experiences. Some team members might get up to speed in a few weeks, others in a few months.

Sit down with your team and ask them what questions they would like to be asked to feel visible, cared for and important. The 'how-are-you-getting-along?' chats are for them; they'll tell you which questions matter to them. Don't forget to add the key question: What can I do to make things more enjoyable for you?

2. Make deliberate practice an essential part of your special way of doing things

There is a difference between regular practice (the simple act of just doing something without necessarily focusing on its purpose) and deliberate practice (doing something with a focused attention towards a specific goal or improving performance – in our case, delivering landmark experiences).

It is easy to slip into automatic pilot mode and do things out of habit. Daily operations and checklists can make repetitive tasks mundane, and we soon reach a point where we stop thinking about what we're doing, how we're doing it, why we're doing it or where it's leading us. This is particularly easy when you're running for months on end with a very streamlined and stretched team. The main goal becomes getting it done instead of thinking of how it improves performance. If you scored low on Navigation in the ESSENCE scorecard, look at where you and your team have fallen into automatic pilot mode.

The danger with slipping into automatic pilot mode is that these important iterations and repetitive tasks become mindless on a day-to-day basis, and this mindless repetition can easily get you off track in the long run. Our work becomes reactive rather than proactive, as we are not measuring the performance or progress of what we're doing.

With deliberate practice, you ensure that all the learnings from your hotel and your team are being put into practice with a specific goal in mind: to improve performance.

For practice to be deliberate, it needs the following:

- A culture of making mistakes

- Focus: clarity and direction

- Measurement

Culture of making mistakes

In the quest for excellence and ensuring we have happy guests, we foster an environment of 'no failure'. Failures or mistakes in these situations lead to unhappy guests. We unwittingly step into the role of villain, causing our guests more problems instead of being the guide who helps them solve their problems and get the prize. Unhappy guests lead to negative reviews, pulling down our overall ranking.

However, this mindset is actually counterproductive. The only way to ensure your team doesn't make the big mistakes that lead to unhappy guests (and you having to give freebies) is to make mistakes an essential part of how things are done in your hotel.

It is only through making mistakes that your staff can learn what they did wrong and how they can avoid making the same mistakes again and again further down the line. When your team aren't scared to make mistakes, they are free to try to improve their performance. It also encourages them to learn how to do things well.

Focus: clarity and direction

Clarity about why a particular action is important shapes the practice. It is important to remind your team on a daily basis why they do things: what benefit it brings to them as professionals, what benefit it brings to their guests, and why it is the best way of doing things in the hotel. When your team members are clear about why they are doing and learning things, they are more likely to stay committed to doing things according to the big picture.

The direction in which your hotel is headed is an equally important part of your focus. Your team needs to know where they are headed and what direction the hotel is taking. Just as with the 'why', it is important to remind our team of the direction we're taking as we are not always heading for our end goals in a linear fashion. There are times when we need to adapt our current course to get to our end goal. Just as cars need a steering wheel to keep them on the right road to the end destination, so your team needs that steering to stay on track.

Measurement

In System, we created your special way of doing things. In Execution, we prototyped each role in each position in your organisational chart. Part of that process involved detailing what each role was meant to do, what it would be accountable for and what results were expected. In Navigation, we look at how to measure the performance of your staff and your business. We create a performance dashboard for each employee, department and the hotel as a whole, to see how we are performing against objectives.

When your team members can see their individual or collective progress, they have a benchmark that helps them keep in mind the big picture and the rationale for why they are doing things. This in turn prevents the small, seemingly insignificant actions from becoming mindlessly repetitive.

You create the dashboard by monitoring the key performance indicators (KPIs) that are relevant to your hotel. These can be financial (e.g., spa occupancy, average treatment rate and guest capture rate) or non-financial (e.g., staff satisfaction, staff wellbeing and guest satisfaction).

When you measure and monitor performance against your gyroscope and the winning plan, you need to keep the big picture present in the day-to-day of your operations, and keep close to your avatar.

EXERCISE 14
MAKE DELIBERATE PRACTICE THE NORM

Keep your team and yourself aligned with your gyroscope.

Open the **Course Correction Canvas** from Exercise 13, click on the tab 'Deliberate Practice' and let's dive in:

1. With your team, brainstorm how you can make mistakes part of the learning process. What are the common mistakes your team members tend to make (identify these without blame and finger pointing)? Why are these mistakes so common? How can team members learn from their mistakes without compromising guest satisfaction? Incorporate your observations into your special way of doing things.

2. With your heads of department, identify the critical points where your teams would appreciate being reminded why they are doing certain tasks. What

would help them see the immense value in doing these actions? Incorporate your observations into your team's onboarding plan.

3. Carefully study which KPIs would be useful to add to your dashboards. Do these KPIs align with your gyroscope? How do they help you and your teams know you are delivering landmark experiences? Incorporate your observations into your hotel's business performance dashboard.

4. Observe all the glitches, and pinpoint which ones are part of the team's learning process and which are part of your offering or system. Separate the team glitches from the offering or system glitches.

In the next step I will show you how to iterate your offering.

3. Build in strategic iteration to your monthly business performance reviews

Strategic iteration is the process of fine-tuning or tweaking your wellness offering to improve the delivery of your landmark experiences. This does not mean constantly changing your system and processes; instead, you should carefully listen to and observe your guests' behaviour and use that knowledge to strategically improve the small but important things in your offering and processes that will enhance the guests' experience, make your staff's jobs easier and prevent you from making hasty and costly decisions.

Let's take the following example. You introduce fitness accessories (a yoga mat, elastic bands and a set of light weights) in your superior category hotel rooms as part of your in-room wellness offering. After a few months of implementation, you notice the accessories have hardly been used. A natural conclusion based on this lack of use would be that the offering was not successful, and the knee-jerk reaction would be to look at Band-Aid solutions that were potentially more expensive, but more on trend and appeared flashier– for example, a static bike. You start again and repeat the cycle.

When we don't strategically iterate our offering, the above vicious cycle becomes common practice. We assume that once we introduce the accessories, our job is done; we assume our guests will automatically love them. However, introducing them is actually when our job begins. It is when we need to keep our ear to the ground, listening to and observing our guests; what are they saying and doing?

TOP TIP 10

You will rarely nail your offering the first time round. You will need to continuously iterate it to get it right and keep it right.

To break the vicious cycle, you have to accept that rarely will you nail it the first time round. You will need to iterate your offering until you get it right. You do this by asking the pertinent questions and tweaking things. In most cases, it is the smallest things that make the biggest differences.

Referring back to the example:

- Are the accessories visible?

- Do guests have to move heavy furniture to roll out their mat?

- Do guests need a mirror to see how they're doing their exercises?

- Is it comfortable for guests to work out in the room? If not, how can we make it comfortable?

- If a novice were to use the accessories, would they know how to do it?

- Is there an accessory missing that would substantially improve the workout experience?

These are small details that have quite simple and easy solutions. For this process to work, careful communication between departments is key. For example, the housekeeping team could be prompted to check how they are finding the in-room wellness accessories the next day. Are guests using them? If so, where are they leaving them? Are they using any pieces of furniture as props to help them exercise? These are cues we need to look for daily so that we can act upon them to enhance guests' experiences.

In Story and System, we couldn't account for every small detail, because at that stage we lacked the key information we have today that could substantially improve the guest experience – guest and staff feedback. It is this vital piece of information we're looking for in Consistency. Eleonore Astier-Petin makes a good case for constantly yet strategically iterating your offering in my *Wellness in Hospitality* interview series. You can read the article here:

www.linkedin.com/pulse/wellness-hospitality-interview -eleonore-sonal-uberoi

Here is how you use guest and staff feedback to fine-tune your offering.

Daily huddles

These are not the same as the standard morning briefings at most hotels where we read off a laundry list: the arrival of a VIP guest, details of a guest complaint, a press trip, and so on. I'm not saying these aren't important topics to cover; they are, but they need a purpose. These daily huddles are conducted with the winning plan kept in mind – how can we better solve our hero's wellbeing problems and deliver the landmark experience? How are we going to make our guests feel special?

This subtle but important shift in how we conduct our daily briefings and morning huddles substantially increases their effectiveness. It prevents us from slipping into the mindless activity of checking off our laundry lists, and encourages us to focus instead on the important big-picture actions.

Review of daily opportunities for improvement

The purpose of these sessions is to identify opportunities for improvement that link back to the gyroscope and the winning plan.

In the example of the in-room fitness accessories, let's assume that one rainy day the housekeeping attendant finds muddy shoe stains on the bench by the bed. The guest had gone for a run and then used the bedroom bench for his step ups. We provided the accessories, but hadn't considered that guests would need a bench. In the daily review, your team suggests including shoe covers and a bath mat in the accessory basket for guests to use. Both of these suggestions are low cost and already available in the hotel, and they align with the gyroscope and your winning plan. We continue to be the guide instead of becoming a villain and causing our guests additional problems (they can't keep up their exercise routine while at the hotel etc.).

Review of daily success stories

It is equally important to know what things are working and what your guests are enjoying.

For example: following the suggestion from the daily huddles, you introduce both the bath mat and the shoe covers, but the housekeeping attendant goes the extra mile and leaves a heavier pair of dumbbells with a hand-written note 'especially for you so you can take your training up a notch today'. The guest is so happy that he asks to know the attendant's name, leaves a great review and shares a picture of the note on his social networks.

These are the kind of success stories— actions that are small and seemingly insignificant but have a big impact on your avatar's journey and their landmark experiences— that should be shared every day. When you share these positive stories, you elevate the energy and morale of your team and encourage them to do more of these actions.

EXERCISE 15
STRATEGICALLY ITERATE YOUR CONCEPT

Fine-tune your concept in a strategic way.

Open the **Course Correction Canvas** from Exercise 13, click on the tab 'Strategic Iteration' and let's dive in:

1. Together with your team, discuss the ideal agenda to follow in the daily huddles. Keep in mind the need to identify areas of improvement and brainstorm solutions as a team.

2. Share success stories – what is working? Once you've finalised the agenda, implement short daily huddles of 20–30 minutes.

3. With the important feedback from the daily huddles, identify the improvements that need to be implemented. Before making any changes to the system or offering, ask yourself:

   • How does this change make the winning plan better?

   • Is this change necessary?

   • Is there anything we're missing?

   • Is this change aligned with the gyroscope and story?

In Navigation, you're fine-tuning and tweaking the small details that make the experience of your guest that much better. You're also making your life easier. You don't fall into the trap of constantly changing your offering, training staff on the new offerings, upsetting guests because you get things wrong, or upsetting your owners by buying things that don't work. After I work with my clients on this stage, they are confident that the changes they make are enhancements that make their special way of doing things in their hotel even better.

CASE STUDIES

Let's take a look at the two case studies and see the Navigation stage in action. Hotel Innovator followed the principles in Navigation and successfully managed to keep its concept on track and systematically iterate parts of the offering that didn't work, thereby saving thousands further down the road. Hotel Traditionalist got sidetracked by the latest equipment, trending therapy and wellness guru and went off track, incurring substantial costs in finding new solutions instead of fine-tuning areas that weren't working.

CASE STUDY
(WHEN THINGS ARE DONE RIGHT)

HOTEL INNOVATOR

The challenge

We passed the critical 3 to 6 months post-opening and ironed out the typical teething problems. The concept was working very well, and the guests loved it, but there was a weak link between the fitness-oriented wellness activities and the spa. The challenges were firstly to ensure we stuck to the concept instead of getting seduced by the new wellness trends, and secondly to fine-tune the areas that weren't working instead of jumping to the wrong conclusions.

The approach

The team didn't have previous experience in luxury or hospitality, so it was important to differentiate glitches in the concept from glitches related to the team's learning process. We firstly tackled the team glitches by creating tailored onboarding and refresher training plans for all staff, depending on their previous experience, strengths and weaknesses. The regular informal individual chats helped us keep track of how team members were getting along and what areas they were struggling with.

After the team became confident in delivering landmark experiences, we could see the glitches in the offering. For example, some of the popular requests from the familiarisation trips included detox and weight loss programmes with detailed lifestyle consultations by doctors. A recurrent topic from our daily huddles was that spa therapists weren't able to offer their guests the more complete wellness experience they were demanding.

The only people asking for detox and weight loss programmes, in fact, were journalists. It would have been tempting to change the entire Spa Sommelier concept five months after opening to respond to the requests of journalists who were trying the latest therapies from other parts of the world. However, we realised that with only small tweaks in the current offering, we could cater to our guests' popular demand for a more complete wellness experience. We knew that our avatar was not looking for a full-on wellness programme when they came to stay at our hotel. We were also aware that such a change would mean a pivot, perhaps requiring specialist skills we couldn't afford. So we decided to offer something more fun and playful; with the Tanita, we measured guests' body mass index and the personal trainer gave them simple but helpful wellness tips to improve their health.

The outcome

Our guests were happier as they could continue with their personal training sessions and have a quick five-minute fitness assessment while away from home. Our team was confident and felt assured that top management knew what they were doing. The general manager felt more confident and in control of the wellness concept. While he could recognise the great new trends that were emerging, he was also aware that not all of them were relevant to his hotel. Fixing the small glitches in the concept instead of completely changing it saved the hotel thousands of dollars.

CASE STUDY
(WHEN THINGS ARE DONE WRONG)

HOTEL TRADITIONALIST

The challenge

The wellness guru had already left a few weeks after opening due to differences in opinion. The hotel finally managed to get a relatively stable wellness team on board around six months into the opening. However, they struggled to rein in the team and the different stakeholders among the chaos of daily operations. Their main challenge was to steer the ship in the right direction when there were so many different directions to follow.

The approach

Everyone tried their best to get the wellness concept up and running, which made their approach reactive. They constantly changed their services menu to make it more exciting, trying to differentiate themselves from the rest and thus pull in custom. When they saw that a new treatment wasn't as popular as they had expected, they quickly removed it and added a new one, and the vicious cycle continued.

For example, their two leading brands had fantastic treatments in world-class spas, but they were both foreign brands, new in Spain. All their training material and marketing collateral was in English and adapted to an international market, making language and cultural differences an important barrier. The new staff didn't understand the training manuals, nor could they communicate with the suppliers when they needed new products or help, which made selling those brands difficult. They felt more comfortable and confident selling the Spanish brands because they could explain the benefits of the products and treatments to guests.

Because the top foreign brands weren't selling, the owners hastily jumped to the conclusion that they weren't well received in their market and searched for new brands. New treatments from different brands were scattered throughout the menu to see what would catch. In fact, the lack of sales had a simple solution all along: to work around the language and cultural barrier. But as the team was too scared to let the owners know, and the owners were too busy trying to find the magic new product or treatment that would transform their wellness business, they didn't stop to analyse and tweak what could easily be fixed.

The outcome

The staff felt confused, insecure and uncomfortable, because they couldn't keep up with all the changes and they didn't know how to perform many of the new treatments. The owners and general manager were frustrated and on edge, constantly on the lookout for the next big trend that would hopefully work for them. They had spent thousands on Band-Aid solutions that didn't work, which fostered a lack of confidence in the capacity of their wellness offering to generate decent returns. They had tried so many new things that they didn't know what else to do, while the wellness offering continued to underperform and bleed money.

CONCLUSION

Hotel operations are works in progress that require constant tweaking and fine-tuning to adapt to rapidly evolving market needs and ensure things run smoothly. It is this constant innovation that keeps your hotel one step ahead. However, when things don't seem to be going as expected, traditional hoteliers get desperate, make hasty decisions and jump into huge investments– for example, purchasing the latest equipment– instead of looking into why the offering isn't working and making the necessary adjustments, which often tend to be small. And when this new equipment doesn't work, they repeat the vicious cycle, each time leaving their staff more lost and their owners more disappointed and less confident in their general manager's judgement.

Innovative and forward-thinking hoteliers create a system whereby they regularly collect feedback from both their staff and their guests on what is working and what is not; once they have all the necessary information, they make small yet strategic adjustments to improve their offering. As a result, they don't spend large sums and confuse their teams or owners by completely changing their offering further down the road. Innovative and forward-thinking hoteliers create a growth environment where their teams feel safe making mistakes, correcting them and learning from them so that they can develop and improve. These hoteliers are respected and appreciated by their teams, guests and owners because they're empathetic, patient and smart in their decision-making.

KEY TAKE-HOMES

1. Innovative and forward-thinking hoteliers understand that their business will be off track most of the time. They know their operations are works in progress that require constant fine-tuning to continue to deliver the landmark experiences.

2. They use their gyroscope from Expectation to help nudge themselves and their teams back on track and to keep the big picture in mind.

3. It is the small, seemingly insignificant actions that are easy to do, but also easy not to do, that keep you on track. You prevent these actions from becoming mindless repetition (and therefore easy to skip) by creating an environment of intentional learning, deliberate practice and strategic iteration.

4. The Navigation environment helps you systematically fix minor faults in your offering and operations so they don't become bigger problems that are costly to correct further down the road or cause you to hastily jump into the wrong investment.

5. Navigation ensures you adapt quickly and easily to changing market conditions, thereby future-proofing your business.

CHAPTER 11
CONSISTENCY

The previous stage, Navigation, was about course correction. It was about taking those small, seemingly insignificant actions to nudge your operations and offering back on track and align them with the gyroscope you created in Expectation and the winning plan in Story. You learned the culture of intentional learning, deliberate practice and strategic iteration. Navigation was about keeping your big picture present – the bird's eye view.

In the next stage, Consistency, we zoom in to your day-to-day operations and ensure you're consistently delivering your guests landmark experiences, each and every time. We take a ground-level view of your wellness offering.

WHAT IS CONSISTENCY ABOUT?

Consistency is about searching for patterns of mistakes and failures in your day-to-day operations and putting the necessary checks in place to foolproof your processes. It is about avoiding human error by pre-empting blunders so that your team can concentrate on being as brilliant as possible, every step of the way. In Consistency, you ensure each member of staff has the critical information they need, when they need it, that they have communicated with all the relevant people, and that they are all systematic and methodical instead of irrational and erratic in their decision-making. Consistency is about increasing the quality of your landmark experiences without increasing the level of expertise of your team.

In Consistency, we create checks to pre-empt service blunders.

WHY IS CONSISTENCY IMPORTANT?

We all know how hard it is to achieve excellence in service standards, but we also know it is even harder to maintain these standards of excellence.

Just as, in Navigation, we looked for the vital guest and staff feedback we didn't have in the Story and System stages to tweak our offering, in Consistency we look for those patterns of mistakes and failures in daily operations we weren't aware of when we were in the Story and System stages.

Consistency is important because it:

- Avoids complacency in your teams and operations

- Ensures your guests are happier because they live their landmark experiences, each and every time

- Ensures your wellness concept is seamlessly integrated throughout the guest journey

- Ensures your team is thorough, efficient and working in synergy

- Saves you money correcting mistakes that are potentially costly and made repeatedly

- Makes your hotel more efficient and effective. In tough times, like the pandemic, this gives your offering an edge over the rest.

When you get Consistency wrong, you accept that blunders in service are inevitable in operations, that they're a norm of the hospitality industry. To achieve perfection in your operations, you fall into the trap of making your team proficient in fire-fighting – successfully handling angry guests and bending over backwards to accommodate guest requests in order to prevent negative reviews. In the end, you have a team that is mistreated by guests, custom that isn't your ideal demographic, and guests who are unhappy as you unwittingly step into the villain role by creating obstacles for them (and your team).

HOW DO YOU GET CONSISTENCY RIGHT?

The key tool that ensures consistency in the delivery of landmark experiences is the checklist.

Checklists are an important tool in improving productivity and consistency in service standards because they remove human error. Industries like aviation and construction, where the stakes are high when it comes to the impact of human error, use checklists extensively at every key stage to flag important points, reminding and prompting the different teams involved.

The hotel industry is known for having well-established SOPs to ensure each department functions optimally. Hotels make regular use of checklists in certain areas (e.g., opening and closing procedures), but rarely do they have customer journey checklists that cohesively involve all departments.

This is partly because, in the hospitality industry, we rely on our people to manage our guests' journeys, as we believe they know how to deal with guest problems. The other reason is that the stakes in our industry are relatively low: we aren't directly saving lives. The worst that can happen due to human error is that the hotel becomes the villain and causes its guest an additional set of problems, and as a result the guest gets a broken experience (which many hoteliers still believe can be fixed by a free treatment). But the broken experience does incur a cost: an opportunity cost.

Checklists are helpful to prevent these fragmented experiences, because they replace guesswork on critical steps and priorities with the clarity and confidence your staff need, particularly in unexpected situations.

For example, in one of my projects the wellness offering included mountain and electric bikes that guests could use to discover the beautiful grounds of the hotel and its surroundings. The terrain was relatively flat and easy; however, there was one slope that had a tricky gradient. A family of four wanted to use the bikes. This was quite a routine service with a routine process– except that the butler on duty missed one small but important step, which was to warn the family of the tricky slope and stony terrain. He assumed that, because the father practised sport and biked often, he didn't need to tell him something that appeared quite obvious. The family went off on their bikes, and when they reached that tricky slope, the father went racing down it.

He wasn't dressed in his biking gear and wasn't as alert as he would have been had he been exercising. He hit a small stone that sent him flying off his bike, metres ahead. He hurt his chin and needed to be taken to hospital, where he got seven stitches. As a result of the accident, the family had to cancel their onward trip.

This was an unfortunate incident that went terribly wrong. However, had that check been put in place, and we highly recommended the use of helmets, we could have at least warned him of the slope so that he might have exercised the necessary caution.

The purpose of checklists

Checklists do not, and should not, tell your team what to do. They are not SOPs. Instead, they help your teams to be as smart as possible, every step of the way. They ensure your team have the critical information they need, when they need it; that they have talked to all the relevant people; and that they are systematic about their decision-making.

The purpose of checklists is to improve the outcome (the quality of the landmark experiences you deliver to your guests) without increasing the level of expertise of your team. I'm not saying you shouldn't increase your team's skill level; what I'm saying is that there is a smarter way to ensure consistent delivery of quality services without making your team expert fire-fighters. Checklists are important because they free your team from thinking about the simple, unimportant details so they can concentrate on the work they want to do and love doing – delivering guests' landmark experiences.

"

CHECKLISTS DO NOT, AND
SHOULD NOT, TELL YOUR TEAM
WHAT TO DO

"

When checklists don't work

Checklists are a valuable tool; however, there are times when they don't work and are met with strong resistance from your team. Checklists don't work in the following situations:

- **When they are used to police the work of your team.** Many hotel managers and heads of department mistakenly use checklists as a tool to police or reprimand their team members. They use checklists to make sure their team members are doing those small niggly tasks that need to be done but that the slightly lazier members are perhaps more likely to skip (e.g., that one last check of the changing rooms before they go home, particularly if the last client left 30 minutes after closing).

- **When they're not integrated into your system**. This happens when a new checklist is added in response to a difficult situation (e.g., an unhappy client), but becomes the norm without looking into the why – whether it was due to an isolated incident or an ongoing issue. When your team has to remember different processes, procedures and checklists that do not link with one another, then checklists are no longer effective.

- **When they're not written with a specific purpose or goal in mind.** Staff can be resistant to seemingly 'pointless' checklists. Many might view it as yet another list they need to tick off each day that no one really looks at because supervisors and managers are too busy with daily operations. When your team can't see the value of the checklist, it makes them feel they are wasting their time ticking off items that really don't have any impact on their work.

- **When no ownership or accountability is attached**. When there is no clarity as to who is responsible for which checklist, this leads to confusion and team members all assuming someone else has done it. Just as we saw in Execution, if everyone is meant to check off the tasks, who is ultimately responsible? When accountability isn't attached to the completion of the checklist, the checklist is no longer effective and becomes a source of confusion instead of a useful guide.

- **When they're lengthy, rigid and time-consuming.** Poorly written checklists tend to be unnecessarily lengthy and rigid. They detail each and every step of the process, instead of highlighting the important checks that need to be performed. These checklists tend to be very time-consuming, straitjacketing your team's creativity and hindering their opportunity to really shine at their work. They become laundry lists instead of useful checks that flag areas of potential problems and pre-empt blunders in service.

HOW TO IMPLEMENT CHECKS AND DELIVER CONSISTENTLY

You implement the right checks for your hotel and help your team to deliver the landmark experiences consistently in the following three stages:

1. Search the patterns of mistakes and failures in your guest's entire wellness journey, from pre-arrival to post-departure.
2. Write the relevant master and individual checklists.
3. Assign accountability, implement and periodically review the checklists.

Let's take a closer look at these three points.

1. Search the patterns of mistakes and failures in your guest's entire wellness journey

Even the most experienced and expert of us can gain from searching the patterns of mistakes and failures in our operations and putting the relevant checks in place so we don't keep making these mistakes again and again.

In System, we carefully evaluated the journey your guests and hotel are taking together, and we also brainstormed with your teams the potential problems in delivery of service. We found the best solutions to those problems and included them in your system. In Consistency, we don't change how we do things. Instead, we fine-tune and reinforce our proprietary system by picking up the 10% of mistakes and failures we were unable to anticipate at the stage of writing our system and processes because we didn't have the necessary day-to-day operational feedback at that time.

TOP TIP 11

Look for the patterns of mistakes and failures in those small things in operations that we sometimes leave to common sense, make dangerous assumptions about or that are seemingly obvious – all the things we get complacent about or make errors in judgement about.

The patterns of mistakes and failures that you're looking for are:

Those small things in operations we sometimes leave to common sense or make dangerous assumptions about

For example, a guest doesn't like her room and requests a change in room. The hotel is at near full occupancy so Andy, the receptionist, informs her that they'll get back to her when a room is available. In the meantime, there is a change of shift; Andy assumes that Petra, the receptionist on the afternoon shift, will follow up. But Petra thought Andy was dealing with it, so didn't take any action. As a consequence, no one followed up and the guest got even more upset. By the time they found an upgraded room for her, her trip was already coming to an end. As soon as she left, she posted a negative review.

We have all encountered scenarios where a small oversight led to a very unhappy guest – and the oversight was not due to lack of competence or skill of your staff. These errors have nothing to do with skill or competence; they are perfectly normal human errors that are very easy to make. But they are also very easy to avoid if you have the right checks in place that prevent guesswork, subjective decision-making and dangerous assumptions.

Those seemingly obvious things in operations that we get complacent about or make errors in judgement on

Note that these errors and mistakes aren't part of the learning environment; nor are they due to the mindless repetition we discussed in Navigation, or the potential problems in delivery of the landmark experiences we identified in System. These are patterns of mistakes, failures, oversights and slack that occur due to complacency, when our teams are well trained, know the system and are engaged in their work, but are now comfortable with the processes, knowledgeable, and confident in their work, and therefore start to relax a little. It is when they take their eye off the ball that they overlook details, provoking a series of unfortunate mistakes that negatively impact the delivery of landmark experiences.

The problem with these kinds of errors in judgement is that they have a snowball effect; they tend to lead to another series of errors in judgement by other staff members until what was seemingly an insignificant oversight leads to a very big problem, such as an extremely angry guest who needs to be comped a free treatment or two.

These are the kinds of mistakes, failures and oversights you are trying to pick up during the entire journey of your guests– from before they arrive at your hotel to long after they've left. And just as in System you took a systems-led approach to your hotel's processes, you do the same in Consistency. You are looking out for patterns in mistakes and failures that are actually happening, and also those that are being picked up by your conscientious staff– those team members who pick up the slack of others so that things can function smoothly.

Note that these actions are different from the strategic iteration exercise we did in Navigation. Those actions were related to improving and enhancing the guest experience and the quality of the landmark experiences. We were tweaking parts of our offering that could be improved based on our guests' feedback, areas we had not considered in Story and System. In Consistency, we're specifically looking for patterns of mistakes and failures in daily operations made by your team, rather than areas for enhancing our offering. If you scored low on Consistency in the ESSENCE scorecard, look into the glitches that occur and identify which are made due to your team (human error) and which are caused by your offering.

Note also that this is not a finger-pointing exercise. It is irrelevant who makes the mistake; what is important is to pick up these human errors so we can put the right checks in place to prevent them happening repeatedly.

EXERCISE 16
OBSERVE PATTERNS OF FAILURE

Look out for the common service blunders that are occurring.

Download the **Service Blunder Pre-empter Canvas** from the Wellness Business Essentials Toolkit at: **www.spa-balance.com/wellness-business-essentials-toolkit/**, click on the tab 'Patterns of Failure' and let's dive in:

1. Sit down with each department and identify together what mistakes are being made, where they're being made, how they're made and the impact they have on the overall guest journey. Also ask the team what slack they have to pick up from other departments and what complaints they get from other departments about what they're doing or not doing. Carefully observe personality types and skill sets to make sure you're picking up traits that are slowly converting your hotel into a people-led instead of a system-led business. Your staff are unlikely to be aware they're doing it, but it's only normal; that is the only way most hotel staff have been taught. They don't know otherwise. Jot all the points down.

2. Get your department heads together and review all the points you jotted down on the patterns of mistakes, failures, oversights and slack. Take the **Avatar's Journey Canvas** from Exercise 5 in Story and plot these mistake patterns along the journey (don't forget to consider the pre-arrival and post-departure parts of the journey).

This will give you and your team a holistic, detailed and objective view of all the patterns and what impact they are having on each part of the journey.

2. Write the relevant master and individual checklists

Now that you have carefully identified the patterns in mistakes, failures, oversights and slack and know how and where they impact along your guest's journey, you can work on putting the right checks in place to flag them and prompt your team to prevent them from falling into these patterns again.

TOP TIP 12

The checks you put in place must make sense and fulfil their purpose of facilitating your team's work, preventing mistakes and increasing the success rate in delivering landmark experiences consistently.

For your checklists to be effective, they must have a what, a who and a why; you must consider what they're for, who they're for and why they're important.

Let's take a closer look at these key elements.

What?

Look at the mistakes and failures you mapped out on the customer's entire journey and think about what checks you need to prompt your team at each step of the way.

- What blunders will each checklist prevent?

- What value will it add to your overall system – your unique proprietary way of doing things?

- What benefits will it have for the overall outcome: the landmark experiences?

For example, if you've identified miscommunication as a mistake that causes parents of young teenagers to get angry because they didn't realise the spa is for adults only and now they don't know what to do with their teenage kids, then you want to act. Apart from the notifications you put on your website and on the reservation confirmation, you can add a checklist item where during check-in the receptionist reminds the family that the spa is for the use of adults only, but adds that children under 16 have access to the supervised digital games room. These checks ensure increased communication and reduce the number of angry parents; they'll know their children can't go to the spa, but the kids can spend time in a safe and entertaining place while they go there themselves. This will substantially contribute towards their landmark experience.

Once you have a list of checks, edit down and streamline it. It is important to be mindful of not over-prompting, because it's easy to get carried away and add checks at every turn. I recommend you do various rounds of cutting tasks down to ensure your checks are as streamlined as possible. Keep in mind the benefits of each check and what value it adds to your overall special way of doing things.

Once you are clear about what checks are needed to pre-empt mistakes or failures, the next step is to consider who the checklists are for.

Who?

Consider who you are writing these checklists for.

- Which roles will need to follow them?

- Who will be responsible for each list?

- Which areas will be involved?

Although we are used to organising our operations in departments, we saw in Story that our avatar's journey spans every single department. Your checklists will therefore need to cover your avatar's entire journey. You will need two types of checklist:

- The master checklist, which takes a bigger-picture view of all the patterns of mistakes, failures, over-sights and slack.

- The individual checklists that filter down from the master checklist and affect each role and area.

If we go back to our above example – the parents upset at not being able to take their teenagers into the spa – and take a look at the family's entire journey from before they get to the hotel until long after they leave, the master checklist will have checks at key touchpoints of their journey to pre-empt those parents getting annoyed. Their ultimate problem is keeping their children happy and occupied. At the reservation confirmation stage, a useful check could be to make sure the teenagers fill out their likes and dislikes form, or a note to inform the parents of activities children can do that don't require parental supervision. Once in the hotel, the games room could be included in the hotel tour; a subtle suggestion to the parents to book their hydrothermal circuit could then be linked to an opportunity to sign their children up for their chosen supervised activities at the same time.

The master checklist would cover all the patterns of mistakes so as to improve the outcome of the journey: the landmark experiences. This master checklist would then be split into each area (rooms, wellness, activities etc.), ensuring that the next step in each checklist cannot be started until the previous one has been checked.

Once you have identified what checks are needed to prevent the mistakes and failures, and who they apply to, the next step is to consider why they are important. (At this point, we are still in the process of defining the necessary checks.)

Why?

To further streamline the checklists, we delve into the why.

- Why is each of these checklists important?

- Why do we need it?

- Why this checklist and not another?

This step is key– not only for you, but also for your team. They, too, need to know why each checklist is important and how it can make their lives easier and less stressful.

Consider why each one of the master and individual check-lists is important and why you need it. Why this particular checklist and not another? Do these checks really improve the outcome consistently, ensuring the delivery of landmark experiences each and every time?

Going back to our previous example, one checklist item could be to make sure parents of young teenagers are constantly reminded that their children can't use the spa. However, a better option would be to thoughtfully recommend activities their young teenagers *can* do. Each checklist is important because it helps to prevent parents of young teenagers becoming upset; however, the one that focuses on suggesting alternatives, that highlights what these young teenagers can do, is more effective than the one that keeps stressing what they can't do. By explaining why it is important to complete these checks, you show your staff that it makes their lives easier – they will have fewer angry guests to deal with in the spa.

This is the level of detail you need so you are confident that each checklist you have is the right one to help prevent the pattern of mistakes you identified in the previous section.

EXERCISE 17
WRITE YOUR CHECKLISTS

Write your master and individual checklists.

Open the **Service Blunder Pre-empter Canvas** from Exercise 16, click on the tab 'Checklists' and let's dive in:

1. Write your first drafts of checklists. Take the journey you plotted – all the mistakes, failures, oversights and slack – and sit down with your team to look at what checks you could put in place to prevent them.

2. Take these checklists and start streamlining them down against the what, who and why:

    • What mistakes, failures, oversights and slack will each checklist prevent?

    • Who is each checklist for?

    • Why is each checklist important? Why this checklist and not another? You should end up with a further streamlined set of checklists that you are confident are the best ones.

Assign accountability, implement and periodically review the checklists

Once you are clear what checklists you need, who they are for and why they are important, the next step is to look at the how.

- How will these checklists be implemented?

- How do they prevent the common mistakes, failures, oversights and slack?

- How will they facilitate your team's job and success rate in delivering landmark experiences?

In this final step, we think about how these checks prevent the failures, mistakes, oversights and slack we saw in the first section, and how they will be implemented. Will there be a list that the relevant staff need to tick on a daily basis? Or is it something they only need to do on certain occasions? The more time you spend on this process, the more effective, useful and successful your checks will be.

For example, in the case of the parents with teenagers, to prevent them from getting angry you might create a master checklist specifically for the entire journey of parents with teenagers, with flags of where potential misunderstandings could arise. You would create the relevant prompts that help solve the parents' problem of keeping their teenagers entertained, then incorporate a series of departmental checks that the staff on duty need to manually complete on a daily basis (and sometimes more than once a day).

Next, assign the right role (not person) to be accountable for each of the checklists – whichever role is the best fit to be responsible for following the particular checklist. Their job is not to police the process– it is to ensure the best possible outcome for your guests: quality landmark experiences that are consistently delivered each and every time. For example, you may identify the role of head of operations as the one responsible for ensuring that the master and individual checklists are being ticked, but they may achieve this by double-checking with the families that they're enjoying their stay, instead of policing each department to check whether the list is ticked off.

Lastly, periodically review the checklists. Your guests' needs are constantly evolving, which means your operations must evolve equally quickly (if not quicker) to adapt and respond to the rapidly changing market conditions. As your operations adapt to create new landmark experiences for your guests, the mistakes, failures, oversights and slack that your team makes will also change over time. You will therefore need to repeat steps 1 and 2 on a regular basis.

You will need to regularly revisit and tweak your checklists to ensure they are still relevant and effective for the new patterns of mistakes and failures. For example, perhaps the games room is now so popular that you are getting requests to add more items and find a bigger space. With these new demands, the patterns of failures and mistakes will change, and the previous checks might not be valid or might need updating to take the new area into account.

Just as your operations and offerings are constant works in progress, so are the checks that you need to put in place to facilitate your team's job and ensure your guests get their landmark experience, each and every time.

EXERCISE 18

IMPLEMENT YOUR CHECKLISTS

Consider how you'll implement the necessary checks.

Open the **Service Blunder Pre-empter Canvas** from Exercise 16, click on the 'Implementation' tab and let's dive in:

1. Take each of your checklists from Exercise 17 and, together with your team, assign the most relevant role to be accountable for each checklist. Remember that these roles ensure the best outcome – the delivery of landmark experiences each and every time.

2. Assign the most relevant role to be accountable for each checklist. Remember that these roles ensure the best outcome – the delivery of landmark experiences each and every time.

3. Periodically review your checklists to see whether they are still effective and whether there are new patterns of mistakes that affect the final outcome.

Your checklists don't need to be long and exhaustive to be effective. They need to be strategic, well thought out and easy to follow. When you take into account the who, what, why and how, your checklists will help prevent these patterns of errors and substantially improve the end result without you having to add any extra skill.

You can download some examples of checklists I use with my clients in the Wellness Business Essentials Toolkit here **www. spa-balance.com/wellness-business-essentials-toolkit/.**

CASE STUDIES

Let's take a look at the two case studies and see the Consistency stage in action. Hotel Innovator followed the principles in Consistency, identifying the patterns in mistakes and failures and putting the right checks in place to preempt these situations and ensure consistency in the delivery of landmark experiences. Hotel Traditionalist accepted that blunders were part and parcel of daily operations and therefore hired staff who were proficient in fire-fighting. This helped to reduce the number of guest complaints, but it didn't improve the quality of their experiences.

CASE STUDY
(WHEN THINGS ARE DONE RIGHT)

HOTEL INNOVATOR

The challenge

In Navigation, we had already implemented the lean mindset– the culture of intentional learning, deliberate practice and strategic iteration to align ourselves with our gyroscope: the Spa Sommelier concept.

However, we were still making a few mistakes. Our team was slipping in regard to small details, which led to unhappy guests and also unhappy therapists, as guests were demanding treatments at times when our therapists weren't available. Some clients also complained about the quality of treatments – they felt rushed, particularly in the evenings.

The challenge was to ensure we were delivering landmark experiences consistently.

The approach

We got together with all departments to look at where our mistakes were happening and where we were failing along the entire guest journey, from pre-arrival to post-departure.

We found that one of the main triggers of the mistakes was guests not booking their treatment or wellness activity upon making a reservation at the hotel. This meant that neither our guests nor our staff knew the itinerary until the guests arrived (remember these people already had a jam-packed agenda). When guests finally decided on their treatments, they wanted them late in the evening – and once they were in the treatment rooms, finally relaxing after their long day, the majority asked for extra time on their massage. These guests also didn't want to leave the spa straightaway after their treatment; they wanted to continue to relax in the hydrothermal area. This in turn meant that the guests went late for their dinner reservations, which had a knock-on effect on their dawn wellness activities (most didn't wake up on time). The hotel incurred additional costs for the personal trainers who had to travel 30 kilometres only to find their clients were a no-show.

One of the key checks we added was that three days before check-in, when we confirmed the guest's transfer to the hotel, we asked a simple question: when would they like to book their wellness experience? This check was included in the Wellness Director's responsibilities, where she would check the new bookings report against the future wellness reservations report. That way we were fully aware of who had booked a treatment beforehand, who wasn't sure whether they would want a treatment, and who was not at all interested. This allowed the team to plan the guest experience proactively instead of reactively.

The outcome

The staff were happy. The therapists didn't need to come in on their day off or stay late, worrying about who would pick up their children from daycare. I was successful in showing the general manager that such uncertainty in shifts did not have to be the norm in the hospitality industry – there was a better way of doing things for his guests, staff and hotel.

The guests were happy, too, because they could enjoy their treatment and laze in the spa for longer without stressing out about being late for their dinner reservation.

CASE STUDY
(WHEN THINGS ARE DONE WRONG)

HOTEL TRADITIONALIST

The challenge

As we saw in the previous five stages– Expectation, Story, System, Execution and Navigation– the team was thrown into a constant state of chaos, having to put out fires on a daily basis. As improvisation was the norm and delivering an experience in itself was a win (irrespective of its quality), the challenge was trying to achieve some sort of consistency when each staff member was doing the best they could given the tools they had.

The approach

For the owners and the general manager, chaos was the norm in hotel operations. They believed that hospitality wasn't for the faint-hearted, and that mistakes and service blunders were part and parcel of daily operations.

To reduce the number of service blunders and to increase their guests' satisfaction, they hired staff who were proficient at fire-fighting, even if they were more expensive. They wanted people who were great at improvising and just delivering. They also invested in expensive training on how to better manage difficult guest complaints. This only equipped their team to handle difficult situations and angry guests better, instead of pre-empting these unfortunate incidents.

Recurrent complaints in the spa were that different guests weren't receiving the same massage, even if they had booked the same one, and that treatments rarely started on time (in some cases, they were also cut short). This was largely due to the fact that the spa had minimal staff on the payroll and relied heavily on external freelance therapists (who hadn't been trained on the spa's menu) to perform treatments at weekends and during the peak season.

The delayed or truncated treatments could have been fixed by putting a check to add at least 10 minutes before and after the treatment so the therapist had enough time to clean the treatment room and prepare for the next treatment. The lack of consistency in treatment quality could have been resolved by adding a check to ensure the freelance therapists had been trained on the treatment, or to limit them to being booked for customised massages only.

Their approach to increasing quality of service was to increase skill in managing unhappy guests instead of putting the right checks in place to prevent them from getting unhappy in the first place.

The outcome

Their strategy helped them keep angry guests quiet, but not satisfied. Staff members were burnt out and turnover was high. The general manager felt he didn't have a 100% grip on the operations; things were good one day and then chaotic another, and although they reached the target guest satisfaction, it was a constant battle. He also struggled to reach revenue targets as he found himself having to offer free treatments to guests. There were days where he found managing the hotel draining and sometimes not worth it. Meanwhile, the owners wondered if they'd ever find a strong enough general manager to cope with their unique and complex business.

CONCLUSION

No matter how perfect your systems or skilled your people, there will always be things that go wrong in operations. There will always be an incident or guest reaction that you would not have planned for.

You can't control or plan for every situation.

However, traditional hoteliers rely heavily on the skill of their people to manage these unexpected incidents. They spend a lot of time and money training their teams to make sure no guest leaves unhappy. As a result, they end up giving free treatments, losing revenue or incurring more costs to ensure they don't get a negative review. Their staff are left feeling undermined, humiliated and demotivated because angry guests bypass them and go straight to managers who succumb to their demands. The traditional hoteliers are constantly on their guard, worried about their overall ranking in customer review sites.

Innovative and forward-thinking hoteliers don't leave these incidents to chance; they pre-empt them. They observe the patterns in failures, oversights and slack in their teams and implement the necessary checks to prevent them from repeating the same blunders in the future. They set their teams up for success and as a result, they consistently deliver landmark experiences to their guests. Their teams feel empowered, confident and respected as their guests are delighted and don't need to speak to the manager to get what they want. They save themselves the headaches and worry of getting negative reviews and instead are happier, less reactive and more deliberate in their approach.

KEY TAKE-HOMES

1. It is not easy to achieve excellence, but it is even harder to maintain it.

2. No matter how routine your hotel operation becomes, your guests never will be. There will always be incidents that arise unexpectedly, incidents you couldn't have planned for.

3. Innovative and forward-thinking hoteliers observe the patterns of blunders and slack in their operations and put the right checks in place to help their teams to successfully deliver landmark experiences, each and every time.

4. Checklists do not tell your teams what to do. Instead, they help your team to be as smart as possible, every step of the way, ensuring they have the critical information they need when they need it, that they've talked and communicated with everyone they need to, and that they're systematic about their decision-making.

5. The right checks lead to more efficient operations, happier guests and staff, and a healthier top and bottom line as you no longer need to offer an angry guest a freebie to make up for a blunder in service and avoid a negative review.

CHAPTER 12
ENGAGEMENT

Congratulations on having completed the first six stages of the ESSENCE model. Hotel operations are complex bricks-and-mortar businesses, and you have managed to pivot your business from one that is people-led to one that is systems-led. You have designed a winning wellness concept, which you have stress-tested. You have created your proprietary way of doing wellness, and you have the right team on board that successfully solves your guests' wellbeing problems – without breaking budget! You've also managed to stay on track with your wellness concept, strategically tweaking areas that weren't working, and you've identified the patterns in mistakes and failures in your operations and put in the right checks to pre-empt these service blunders. Your team is happy and consistently delivering landmark experiences, and so your guests are happy too.

The last stage, Engagement, is the icing on the cake that sets your hotel apart from the rest. It keeps you one step ahead of your competitors.

WHAT IS ENGAGEMENT ABOUT?

Engagement is about going that extra mile. It is about repeat custom and rave reviews. It is about how happy and engaged your clients are, to the point that they rave about their experience in your hotel to their family, friends and followers, and they can't wait to come back. In Engagement, we focus on how you can create and prompt these shareable landmark experiences, not because you ask happy guests to share them, but because they really want to. It is about making your hotel shareable and getting exponential in your outreach. This is the stage where you leave your legacy behind – where you make your hotel the landmark in your area.

In Engagement, we create exponential outreach for your hotel.

WHY IS ENGAGEMENT IMPORTANT?

The Engagement stage future-proofs your hotel. It ensures that your hotel not only survives, but thrives– even in the face of adversities. It makes your hotel build a loyal and committed customer base that genuinely engages with your brand and actively recommends it.

Engagement is important because it:

- Secures your hotel as a landmark in its destination in the eyes of your customer

- Results in free publicity as guests share and post about their experiences

- Allows you to explore alternative, non-traditional revenue streams

- Creates a positive atmosphere for your guests and staff

- Increases your profitability through higher revenues and lower marketing and advertising spend

- Makes your stakeholders happier because they enjoy higher returns on investment.

Engagement is important because you look beyond the traditional rooms-centred metrics (revenue per available room, occupancy, rate generation index and market penetration index) to measure performance. You measure your hotel's performance according to the assets your guests engage with. In other words, you measure how shareable your hotel is.

When you get Engagement wrong, you fail to systematically build strategic innovation and creativity into your offering, and you risk ending up with an offering that is obsolete or no longer relevant. You essentially decrease the total value of your hotel's asset ecosystem. As a result, you have guests who don't leave rave reviews and actively recommend your hotel to their networks as much as they could. You therefore have to spend thousands on marketing and advertising spend to tell the world how great your hotel is and to pull in new customers.

HOW DO YOU GET ENGAGEMENT RIGHT?

Today, the cornerstone of a successful hotel is how shareable it is. A hotel that is not shareable has simply not invested correctly in building the right assets.

—— " ——

THE CORNERSTONE OF A
SUCCESSFUL HOTEL IS HOW
SHAREABLE IT IS.

—— " ——

Experiences that don't get shared weren't authentic, meaningful or memorable enough– they were forgettable. For guests to want to share experiences, they have to be engaged with them.

Coronavirus educated us about the R number: the replication factor of a virus, or how many times the virus is shared per infected person. If the number is below one, then the virus will eventually die out. If the number is above one, then it spreads exponentially.

Let's take a look at the following examples:

- If the R number is 3, every 10 infected people will spread the virus to 30 others. These 30 people then spread it to another 90, and so on. We can see how exponential the spread can be in this scenario.

- If the number is 0.7, every 10 infected people will spread the virus to another seven people. These seven then spread it to about five others, and so on. We can see how the spread of the virus will eventually die out in this scenario.

The replication number perfectly illustrates the power of spread, the influence one person potentially has on others.

This influence also applies to the business world, especially the power your customers have to spread the word about how great (or not) their experience at your hotel was. I call this the S number, or the 'shareable' factor.

The 'S' number

Each guest who stays in your hotel has the power to replicate or share their experience at your hotel with their friends, family, colleagues and network. If the shareable factor (its S number) is, say, 10 or 15, it means every guest who stays in your hotel can influence 10 or 15 more people to visit, as well as being likely to want to come and stay again themselves. If your hotel's S number is below one, then the hotel has to spend money to make up the difference with advertising and marketing.

Hotels usually spend between 5% and 9% of their annual revenues on marketing and advertising, on telling people how great they are and convincing people to come and stay. They also invest heavily in ramping up their rating on customer review sites.

It is said that the conversion rate of social media and other digital platforms ranges from about 0.7% to approximately 3%. Hence, for every 100,000 followers who actively engage across all platforms with your hotel and brand, you get between 700 and 3,000 new guests staying at your hotel.

So, if a hotel has an average annual revenue of €5m and 300,000 followers across their social networks, they spend between €250,000 and €450,000 a year (5–9% of total revenue) on getting between 2,100 and 9,000 new guests (the 0.7–3% conversion rate) per year.

If hotels were to move that money towards their 'shareables' budget, ensuring that every single touchpoint in their guest's journey was made shareable, then their success rate would be exponential. Let me explain how, using the example of Hotel A.

Hotel A

Hotel A has 60 rooms and runs on an average occupancy of 60%, an ADR of €250, an average length of stay of two nights and an average of 1.8 persons per room; it maintains a repeat custom percentage of 15%. Its total annual revenue is €5m and it spends 5% of its total revenue on marketing, advertising and PR. It has a total of 300,000 followers across all social media platforms and, as per its agency, its average conversion rate across platforms is about 1%.

- Total number of guests in the hotel per year
  = 11,826 [(60 × 1.8 × 60% × 365)/2]

- Total number of repeat guests in the hotel per year = 1,774 [11,826 × 15%]

- Total number of new guests in the hotel per year = 10,052 [11,826 - 1,774]

- Total marketing, advertising and PR spend
  = 5% of €5,000,000 = €250,000

- Total number of new guests through this initiative
  = 3,000 [1% × 300,000 followers]

- Baseline of guests (excluding repeat custom)
  = 7,052 [10,052 - 3,000]

- Baseline of guests (including repeat custom)
  = 8,826 [11,826 - 3,000]

- Cost of acquisition per client
  = €83 [€250,000/3,000 new guests] (~33% of ADR)

- Cost per room night
  = €46 [€83/1.8 persons per room] (~18% of ADR)

The hotel needs 11,826 guests in its hotel to reach its budget. Out of these 11,826 guests, 1,774 are repeat guests who return because either they enjoyed their stay or it's convenient for them. It has a baseline of guests (the number of guests it has as a base through various sales and marketing initiatives) of 7,052. Therefore, to reach its target of 11,826, the hotel needs to top up its number of new guests by 3,000 each year, which it does through marketing and advertising. Its baseline of guests, including repeat custom, is 8,826.

The hotel's shareable factor, or S number, is therefore 0.75 (8,826 / 11,826).

In other words, for every 100 guests in their hotel, they pull in 75 new guests. This means that to make up for the deficit of those 25 clients, they need to spend €83 per client, or €46 per room per night.

Now let us look at how different this scenario could look if the hotel shifted its marketing and advertising efforts towards making its guests' experiences shareable.

Let's assume that each person who comes to this hotel has about 2,000 followers across all their social media platforms; each one has the power to influence 2,000 people who know them, either through a close connection or an acquaintance. While these 2,000 people might not all be close friends, they are still people who have some sort of common connection— hence they pass the initial vetting process. In marketing terms, they are likely to belong to the same demographic, with similar values, problems and aspirations (i.e., they are potentially this hotel's target audience). Hence, there is little wastage compared with, for example, advertising in magazines where we don't really know if the reader is in our target market or whether they just picked up the magazine in the hairdresser's to kill time.

Let's imagine these guests are so happy with their experience at this hotel that they each share it with their 2,000 followers. If we take the conversion rate of 1%, this means every happy guest could potentially bring in 20 new guests to this hotel who are looking for that same landmark experience. Hence the 11,826 guests a year could potentially bring in 236,000 guests a year. You can see how exponential the outreach can be if the hotel has the right strategy in place.

Making our guests' experiences special, memorable and shareable doesn't necessarily need to be complicated or expensive.

Let's take a look at examples of the different approaches of two hotels with the Smith family: a family of four with two teenagers, Jake and Anna.

Hotel reactionary

A few days before the family's arrival, Mrs Smith receives a standard reservation confirmation email, which she browses through quickly to see whether she needs to action anything.

On the day, after an eight-hour road trip, they finally arrive at the hotel. They check in, are given a map of how to get around the facilities, and are told that the concierge is at their disposal if they'd like to book any activities.

The next day, the shower in Mr and Mrs Smith's room breaks down. Mrs Smith reports it. After the maintenance guy fixes it, it works for a few minutes but then breaks down again. Disappointed, Mrs Smith asks for another room, but there are no other rooms of that category available. Irritated, she asks to speak to the manager who, clearly noticing her disappointment, offers her a free treatment of her choice at the spa. She was already planning to treat herself during her stay, but now she doesn't need to pay for it! Mrs Smith gladly accepts, but soon gets upset because all the spa therapists are fully booked at the time she wants. Worried Mrs Smith will leave a negative review, the general manager asks one of the therapists to stay late to perform the treatment. Tired after an eight-hour shift and five deep tissue massages, the therapist performs Mrs Smith's treatment to the best of her abilities. Mrs Smith would have loved to add another 15 (paid) minutes to her massage, but notices that the massage is being rushed slightly so doesn't ask.

All in all, the family had a good vacation; they spent some quality time together and disconnected from the stresses and strains of everyday life. Although the shower didn't work, Mrs Smith got a free massage! They shared their holiday story with their friends: the broken shower, the free spa treatment, the lovely beach. A typical holiday.

Hotel visionary

Upon reservation, Rose, a receptionist, contacts Mrs Smith via email and requests that each member of the family fill out a quick questionnaire so she can personalise their stay. Every week building up to their arrival, they receive a message with tailored information about the experiences the hotel has to offer, including some wellbeing tips on how to make the eight-hour road trip more comfortable. For Mr and

Mrs Smith, doing nothing sounds like heaven; for Jake and Anna, the fully equipped music room is a dream come true, and they have already started sharing the cool hotel they are going to visit.

By the time they check in, they feel they already know the staff, particularly Rose, and feel completely at home despite the long road trip.

Mrs Smith has the same problem – the broken shower and no available rooms – but she understands that these things happen, as Rose is genuinely apologetic. While the shower is mended, Mrs Smith decides to pay for a treatment in the spa. A therapist who is on shift is delighted to attend her and offers her a 15-minute upgrade. Mrs Smith is delighted and doesn't care that she has to shower in Jake and Anna's room while they are busy being rock stars, recording their TikTok videos in the music room and making their friends jealous.

The Smiths had a fantastic and memorable holiday; Jake and Anna were over the moon at being the coolest kids in school. They spent more than they had planned, but it was worth every single penny. Mr and Mrs Smith shared their experience with their 5,000 friends and followers on Facebook and Instagram, and Anna and Jake had already been sharing their journey with their 4,000 friends and followers on Instagram and TikTok. Their friends were already pestering their parents to take them to the hotel Anna and Jake's family had visited.

By keeping this family of four happy, Hotel Visionary targeted four different captive audiences through making the Smiths' stay in the hotel truly special and easy to share.

Hotel Visionary's outreach was a captive audience of 9,000 potential new guests. With a conversion rate of 1%, this family of four potentially brought in 80 new people. Imagine if another handful of families lived the same experience? That's exponential!

TOP TIP 13

Invest the 5–9% you spend on marketing and advertising on making each and every aspect of your guests' journey with your hotel shareable.

The forward-thinking and innovative hotels won't spend 5–9% on telling people about who they are and how wonderful they are. Instead, they invest that 5–9% in the hotel itself, in making every single aspect of their hotel shareable so that their guests tell the world how great the hotel is.

HOW TO MAKE EVERY ASPECT SHAREABLE

So how do you make every single aspect of your hotel shareable so that your guests want to rave about their landmark experience? Here's how.

1. Calculate your hotel's 'S' number and add it to the KPIs on your business performance dashboard

The first step is to know what your 'S' number, or shareable factor, is.

To calculate your shareable factor, you need the below information at hand. I've used the figures from Hotel A to work through the example with you.

Hotel A statistics:

- Total number of hotel rooms = 60

- Hotel occupancy = 60%

- ADR = €250

- Persons per room = 1.8

- Average length of stay = 2 nights

- Total number of guests in the hotel (including children) = 11,826

- Total number of repeat guests = 1,774

Marketing statistics (your sales and marketing team should be able to provide this information for you):

- Total number of followers across all social media platforms = 300,000

- Total spend on advertising across all these platforms = €250,000

- Average conversion rate of all platforms = 1%

Calculating your 'S' number:

1. Calculate the total number of guests that stay in your hotel (note: this is not the same as the total number of people in your hotel every night) using the formula below:

(HOTEL OCCUPANCY × TOTAL NUMBER OF ROOMS × PERSONS PER ROOM)/AVERAGE LENGTH OF STAY

- 11,826 [(60 × 1.8 × 60% × 365)/2]

2. Calculate the number of guests that are pulled through your advertising and PR spend using the formula below:

(TOTAL NUMBER OF FOLLOWERS
ACROSS ALL SOCIAL MEDIA PLATFORMS) ×
(AVERAGE CONVERSION RATE OF ALL PLATFORMS)

- 3,000 [300,000 followers × 1%]

3. Calculate your baseline number of guests (including repeat custom). These are the guests your hotel has pulled in through other initiatives, like property-level sales, tour operators, sales offices etc. Use the formula below:

(TOTAL NUMBER OF GUESTS IN YOUR HOTEL) - (TOTAL NUMBER OF GUESTS PULLED THROUGH SALES, ADVERTISING AND PR)

- 8,826 [11,826 - 3,000]

4. Calculate your shareable factor using the formula below:

(BASELINE OF GUESTS INCLUDING REPEAT CUSTOM)/
(TOTAL NUMBER OF GUESTS THAT STAY IN YOUR HOTEL)

- 0.75 [8,826/11,826]

In the above example, the hotel's shareable number is below one, which is quite common to begin with. Getting your shareable number above one takes time and investment in making key aspects of your avatar's journey shareable.

Add your S number to the KPIs that go on your business performance dashboard.

EXERCISE 19

CALCULATE YOUR 'S' NUMBER

Know your hotel's shareable factor.

Download the **S Number Worksheet** from the Wellness Business Essentials Toolkit at **www.spa-balance.com/wellness-business-essentials-toolkit/** and let's dive in:

1. Have all your property and marketing statistics at hand and follow the instructions on the worksheet.

2. Add your S number to your KPI dashboard.

Let's see how you can achieve a shareable number above one for your hotel.

2. Go the extra mile

Forward-thinking and innovative hoteliers understand that they need to go the extra mile to deliver their avatar more than the prize and make their experience truly special. They know they can no longer merely deliver landmark experiences, because that is what their avatars expect as a minimum from their stay at their hotel. When they pay for their stay, guests expect their problems to be solved and to get their prize, so that in itself is not enough for them to want to share their experiences with their networks.

What makes your guests want to happily share their experiences with their networks is when the experience is truly special; when the experience they have lived, as a result of your hotel guiding them through their journey, transforms them or something in their lives.

As emotional beings, we're driven by our desire to transform. We all look for positive change; we all want to be better versions of ourselves in some way, shape or form; for example, we want to look better, perform better, or be happier.

The businesses and brands that actively participate in our identity transformation make us want to engage with them and stay loyal and committed to them. These transformations don't need to be big and life-changing; they can be small, yet still significant or meaningful enough for us to feel better. Examples might be fitting into an outfit you thought you could never fit into, or feeling better or more energised, or having happier relationships as a result of being in a better mood by sleeping better.

When it comes to your hotel, you have the perfect tool to help your guests with their transformation: your wellness offering. Your wellness offering allows you to go the extra mile and deliver more than the landmark experiences. It allows you to actively participate in your guests' wellbeing transformation.

In the Who section of Expectation, we studied our avatar in great detail. In Story, we created the winning plan to guide our guests through their journey to their prize – the landmark experiences. We narrowed down their wellbeing problems into the following four categories: physical, emotional, mental and spiritual. We also briefly touched on their aspirations in these first two stages.

In Engagement, we go a step further and take a deep dive into our avatar's wellbeing aspirations:

- What are their wellbeing desires?

- What version of themselves do they aspire to be?

- Can you help them achieve this 'weller' version of themselves? If so, how?

A good starting point is to study your avatar's social media and other online presence and see what kind of content they share and how they project themselves. Just as you did with their wellbeing problems, you narrow down your avatar's wellbeing aspirations into the corresponding categories: how they desire to look, feel, think and be.

Let's pull out the examples of the wellbeing problems of Hotel Innovator's avatar in Story and add examples of their possible aspirations alongside (in your case, you'd actually find out what your avatar's wellbeing aspirations are):

PHYSICAL PROBLEMS	EMOTIONAL PROBLEMS	MENTAL PROBLEMS	SPIRITUAL PROBLEMS
- *Insufficient exercise*	- *Anger*	- *Anxiety*	- *Lack of purpose*
- *Uncomfortable, stiff body*	- *Frustration*	- *Insomnia*	- *Confusion*
- *Dull, grey skin*	- *Distress*	- *Impatience*	- *Indifference*

HOW THEY DESIRE TO LOOK	HOW THEY DESIRE TO FEEL	HOW THEY DESIRE TO THINK	HOW THEY DESIRE TO BE
- Fit and strong	- Happy - 'In control' of things	- Positively, with can-do thoughts - That they can achieve what they want to	- Successful - Fulfilled - Content

Like the mental and existential wellbeing problems, you will notice that your avatar's aspirations are longer term. It is unlikely you will be able to help your client lose the 10 kilos they are overweight by during their stay at your hotel; nor are you likely to solve their insomnia or anxiety. But the forward-thinking and innovative hoteliers recognise that it is in the aspirations where they can make a more meaningful impact.

EXERCISE 20

GO THE EXTRA MILE

Deliver your avatars more than the landmark experience.

Open the **Extra Mile Canvas** from the Wellness Business Essentials Toolkit and let's dive in:

1. Together with your team, revisit the Who section in your **Wellness Concept Value Canvas** from Exercise 1 and go over your avatar's aspirations.

2. Hire a social media or digital specialist to study a sample of 50 guests' or avatars' social media and online presence. How are they projecting themselves? Who are their friends? How do they want to be perceived? Add this information to the aspirations list.

3. Narrow down the list into the following categories: how they desire to look, feel, think and be. Add these alongside the four categories of wellbeing problems in the **Understand Your Avatar Canvas** from Exercise 4.

3. Curate the shareable moments

You participate in your avatar's wellbeing transformation by incorporating their main aspirations into the key touchpoints you mapped out in their journey in Story and curating moments that are really special and super easy to share.

For example, your avatar's villain is a high-profile C-suite job that causes them to become overweight, stressed and sleep deprived (wellbeing problems). They aspire to be a fit, healthy and balanced person who is successful and also spends quality time with their family and friends. In Story, you mapped out their wellness journey to solve these wellbeing problems along the different touchpoints to their prize (the landmark experience). In Engagement, you go the extra mile by incorporating their aspiration to be fit, healthy and balanced into these key touchpoints of their journey: the pre-arrival and post-departure. For example, you could guide them through their insomnia after they have left your hotel by offering online consultations with one of your visiting practitioners or sending them a book on insomnia. You could also offer wellness tips and suggestions or create a Facebook group or online community where you make it easy for them to engage with your hotel and share their stories. Just as with your wellness concept, you don't need grand or expensive details to participate in your guests' wellbeing transformation; you just need to prolong the timeline for which you engage with your guests. You achieve that by offering services that help them achieve their wellbeing aspirations.

We can see from the above example that the options we have to truly engage with our guests and help them reach their wellbeing aspirations are endless. Many of these options are simple and cheap. They probably don't generate large direct revenues from the actual activities themselves, but they are an important part of your products and services ecosystem and potentially have a substantial impact on your top and bottom lines through the indirect revenues they generate.

When you make your avatar's journey special and shareable, you increase your hotel's S number. You draw in more of your target audience through your happy guests (your avatar's extended network) and increase repeat custom, without having to offer discounted packages to lure in new customers who probably wouldn't have interacted with your brand had it not been for the special deal. You maintain your average rates and save on middleman commission.

If you scored low on Engagement in the ESSENCE scorecard, look at how easy you're making it for your guests to share their special moments.

EXERCISE 21
CURATE THE SHAREABLE MOMENTS

Make it super easy for your guests to share the special moments.

Open the **Shareable Moments Curator Canvas** from the Wellness Business Essentials Toolkit and let's dive in:

1. Together with your team, brainstorm how you can help your guests to achieve their wellbeing aspirations. Focus on the key milestones along your guests' journey: the pre-arrival, arrival and post-departure.

2. Thoughtfully curate these special opportunities for your guests so that it is super easy for them to share with their networks.

Go back to the Winning Plan Canvas from Exercise 6 in Story and incorporate these curated special opportunities into the winning plan.

4. Share your avatar's success stories

To transform your guests' wellbeing, the change needs to be visible. They need to see or feel that something inside them has improved, albeit in a small but nonetheless important way. This change starts before they get to your hotel, and can continue months after they have left it.

You help your guest complete their wellbeing transformation by showing them how their wellbeing, and in turn their life, has changed. For example, if your avatar's wellbeing aspiration was to reach a healthy weight, and through your hotel's wellness advice (e.g., via ongoing online coaching sessions) they reach that healthy weight six months after their stay, show them their progress and celebrate it with them – for example, they can now buy that outfit they never thought they could fit into and see themselves in a whole new light. It is that unparalleled feeling of achievement you want your guests to share.

As humans, we need to see progress. Only when we perceive our progress do we enjoy the sense of achievement. But we are not only drawn to our own progress; we are also drawn to the progress of other people. When we see transformation in others, we want it for ourselves, too.

In Engagement, you show your guests the wellbeing transformation that is possible so they can see it is something they, too, can achieve. You share the success stories of your guests and their journey to wellbeing. You do this by getting genuine testimonials from guests whose wellbeing transformation you have participated in and sharing it on your website and across social media, perhaps inviting them to share their success stories in person (e.g., in a workshop or talk).

The majority of hotels focus on taking pictures of their surroundings, their rooms, their grand spa or their Michelin-star restaurant. They love to showcase how great their hotel looks. However, in the end, they essentially share the features of their hotel rather than what benefits their guests can get from these features.

TOP TIP 14

Focus on the benefits of your hotel's offering instead of the features of your hotel.

Your guests don't care about the features of your hotel as much as you do. They care about the benefits of these features and how your hotel will help them solve their wellbeing problems and noticeably improve their wellbeing. For example, Apple doesn't talk about the iPhone's technical features. Instead, it shares the benefits of the device, of what its customers can do with the iPhone – take better pictures and flashier videos, track their health, improve their productivity, work while on the go, and so on. Apple paints a clear picture of how its customers' lives will look when they buy the iPhone.

In the same way, your guests don't want to know how great the facilities of your hotel are; they are interested in knowing how great they will feel, the amazing things they'll be able to do, and how much better their life will be after their landmark experience at your hotel.

Talk about the benefits your guests get from interacting with your brand. It's ultimately about them – they are the hero. They want to become a better version of themselves after attaining their prize and you need to show them how that is possible.

This is what the last stage of my ESSENCE model, Engagement, is about: to get your guests to genuinely engage with your hotel so they want to share their experiences with their network. It goes beyond the Instagrammable moment or photo of a beautiful dish; it is about sharing how their lives are better as a result of staying at your hotel and interacting with your brand. It is this level of engagement that will help you to future-proof your business. In other words, it allows you to design your business in such a way that it stays relevant and constantly evolves by responding and adapting to changing market conditions. There is no better barometer than your shareable factor to achieve this.

EXERCISE 22
SHARE YOUR AVATAR'S SUCCESS STORIES

Engage with your guests in a meaningful way.

Open the **Success Story Canvas** from the Wellness Business Essentials Toolkit and let's dive in:

1. Together with your marketing team, see how you can talk less about the features of your hotel and more about the benefits.

2. Train your team to show their guests how their lives have changed.

Gather client testimonials and share them with your following (these go beyond five-star reviews).

CASE STUDIES

Let's take a look at the two case studies and see the Engagement stage in action. Hotel Innovator followed the principles in Engagement and opted to make their guests' experience special and super easy to share by curating shareable moments. Hotel Traditionalist approached Engagement incorrectly, opting instead to share how great their hotel was and all the awards it had won.

CASE STUDY
(WHEN THINGS ARE DONE RIGHT)

HOTEL INNOVATOR

The challenge

The hotel was very well received in the market. The PR and marketing efforts were incredibly successful, and the hotel was featured in important publications and shortlisted for various industry awards. However, it was costing the owners a substantial sum. The challenge was to cut part of the advertising spend and divert it to making their guests' experiences truly special and shareable. This was risky, as the hotel was still a young business that hadn't yet built a strong baseline of guests.

The approach

The hotel's concern was the quality of images and videos shared. They wanted the images their guests shared to match their brand's look and feel. Hence their strategy was to create content (beautiful videos and photos) for the hotel's social platforms so that their guests could engage with that content and share it with their networks rather than sharing user-generated content. The problem with this strategy was that the staged photographic content was of impersonal, ad hoc moments instead of real stories of guests' special moments. The hotel soon realised that their and their guests' shared content would eventually drown in a sea of similar content being shared by other hotels, so they agreed to change their approach. We set out to thoughtfully curate personal and shareable photo and video opportunities throughout the hotel.

When we referred back to our avatar's aspirations in Expectation, we saw that one of them was to live culturally enriching experiences; many guests had a love for art, history and interior design. With this aspiration in mind, we revisited the journey we mapped out in Story and identified the key milestones in their journey where we could make it easy and almost intuitive for our guests to share their experiences. One of these was the blind wine-tasting ritual in the spa.

Our guests weren't expecting to have a blind wine-tasting session in the spa, of all places– and they weren't expecting to be doing so while sitting on a Nakashima bench worth hundreds of thousands of dollars with a two-year waiting list. Which other spa could offer that? For many guests, this was a truly special moment. We had successfully curated meaningful content moments; moments that were special and easy for guests to share with their networks. These moments were real stories, not mere pictures.

The outcome

The hotel became a landmark in the region. Over the following six months, it built an engaged, loyal and committed client base who happily shared their experiences with their networks. The positive energy of their guests also made the staff happy and engaged as they saw the results of the landmark experiences. The general manager had achieved his mission of building a performance-driven business that made the owners proud, and he got himself the great exit deal he was looking for. Even today, the legacy we created still prevails.

CASE STUDY

(WHEN THINGS ARE DONE WRONG)

HOTEL TRADITIONALIST

The challenge

In Consistency, we saw how the hotel was struggling to consistently deliver landmark experiences and meet its financial objectives. The challenge was to get a steady flow of new customers to increase sales but without spending thousands on marketing and advertising or dropping rates. Like Hotel Innovator, this was still a young business that needed to increase brand awareness.

The approach

The team promoted how great their hotel and vision were. They shared their story of building a sustainable business that respected its surroundings and community, and used their renowned certification in sustainable building to lure in guests who were environmentally responsible – and who would be forgiving of the small blunders in service, because they knew the business had a greater purpose.

The problem with this strategy was that it made their marketing initiatives about themselves instead of about their guests – and we saw in Story that the guest, not the hotel, should be the hero. They were successful in getting media coverage within the trade press but not so successful within end-consumer publications.

This was partly because their delivery of experiences was inconsistent; some guests shared their disappointing moments, but the general manager ensured they were compensated with a free treatment so they didn't leave a negative review.

The other reason was that the guests' journey through the hotel was not curated in a way that made sharing the special moments easy or engaging. Not all guests left the hotel unhappy; many loved the owners' vision and concept, but they didn't think to share – or they didn't know how to share – their special moments in such a unique hotel. Hence, the hotel missed out on the opportunity to attract more of this type of environmentally conscious guest.

Instead, through the team's compensation strategy, the hotel attracted more of the type of guests who were looking for a good, affordable holiday or escape near the beach instead of guests who shared their vision for sustainable living. These guests weren't specifically going to the hotel due to its strong environmental policy; they merely wanted a good deal and good value for money while being in a beautiful location.

The outcome

The hotel implemented a significant drop in its ADR to attract the typical summer and business custom to drive occupancy levels, which meant lower profits. By attracting the wrong type of guests, they unwittingly positioned themselves as another good, but not amazing, hotel in the region. Eventually, the general manager, frustrated and burnt out with the experience, left to work in a less visionary but more organised company where things were less of an uphill struggle. The owners continued their cycle with the next general manager and even today the hotel still performs below its true potential.

CONCLUSION

The more memorable and special the experiences of your guests, the more likely they are to share their experiences with their networks and pull other people into your hotel. Traditional hoteliers spend their money on advertising and social media influencers to tell everyone how great their hotel is and how wonderful their facilities are. They're happy delivering their guests landmark experiences and they spend thousands to get the most popular influencer, many times reaching out to the wrong audience (that of the influencer). Their teams feel annoyed because they are diverted from serving paying guests to satisfy the several demands of a VIP influencer on a free holiday with their family. Traditional hoteliers feel they can never keep up with the rapidly changing digital marketing platforms.

The innovative and forward-thinking hoteliers get their guests to promote the hotel for them and save thousands of dollars on advertising and influencers. They focus on making each and every guest's experience truly special and shareable, and they actively curate moments that are easy for guests to share with their networks. The staff enjoy their work and feel more involved in the guests' experiences. Innovative and forward-thinking hoteliers don't worry about attracting new customers or suffering the peaks and troughs of seasonal demand. They enjoy the peace of mind a steady flow of business brings, and their owners are delighted with them because they have a brand with a loyal and committed following – a brand that people love and engage with, instead of one that depends on influencer validation.

KEY TAKE-HOMES

1. All humans are driven by transformation. We all aspire to be a better version of ourselves in some way, shape or form.

2. The brands that realise that their customers are emotional beings driven by their aspirations, and that they care more about their desire to be better than about buying a particular product or service, actively participate in their guests' transformation.

3. When we offer our guests the opportunity to transform their wellbeing, we build a truly committed, engaged and loyal client base who want to share their experiences with their friends, family and network.

4. The forward-thinking and innovative hotels won't spend 5–9% on telling people about who they are and how wonderful they are. Instead, they invest that money in the hotel itself, in making every single aspect of their business shareable so that their guests tell the world how great the hotel is.

5. Each guest who stays in your hotel has the power to replicate or share their experience with their friends, family, colleagues and network. Your hotel's 'S' number, or shareable factor, tells you how shareable your hotel is.

PART 4

WHAT INNOVATIVE AND FORWARD-THINKING HOTELIERS ARE DOING

'THE LINES BETWEEN WELLNESS, LEISURE AND BUSINESS TRAVEL WILL SLOWLY DISAPPEAR AS WE ALL GET MORE AND MORE MINDFUL ABOUT OUR WELLBEING.'

- JAIMY ALEXANDER VAN DEN BERG

CHAPTER 13
ESSENCE IN PRACTICE

In the last part of the book, I'd like to share four examples of innovative and forward-thinking hoteliers who successfully pivoted their businesses during the 2020 pandemic by putting wellness at the core of their business strategy. These real-world examples prove that the meticulous application of the ESSENCE principles produces a thriving wellness asset that future-proofs your hotel.

First, we look at Ana Beatriz's experience as a hotel consultant based in Portugal. Ana's firm belief in the role of wellness as the future of hospitality is reflected in every project she tackles. The property her case focuses on is a family-owned 30-key resort in Portugal. Her approach was to weave wellness into the hotel's DNA. The unique wellness-centric offering proved resilient to crisis and thrived during the pandemic while still maintaining high rates.

Next, we examine Fernando Gibaja's experience as a seasoned hotelier managing an emblematic hotel in Singapore.

Responding to the new, wellbeing-conscious demographic that was now buying, Fernando rehauled his hotel's offering to include wellness at its core. Using small, incremental changes to the existing offering, he adopted a lean approach to differentiate his hotel. These subtle changes allowed the hotel to pivot and cater to its ideal long-stay demographic, with a higher average spend per guest and increased social engagement.

The third case study addresses the journey of Abedin Sham, owner and operator of hotels in India and the Middle East. His quest was not only to survive but to thrive. He scrutinised market behaviours and available offerings and discovered an opportunity for growth – a unique local experience for wellness-conscious guests seeking fulfilling hotel stays. This quick response and careful investment in an integrated wellness asset catapulted his 20-key lifestyle hotel to the status of local favourite within the cut-throat market of Mumbai.

Finally, the story of Yagna Prathap lays out a compelling case for medium-sized owning companies and investors looking to protect their portfolio through wellness. As his company's portfolio focused heavily on the business segment (a segment that was no longer buying the way it used to), Yagna pitched to shift investment focus to the new corporate market: wellness. By incorporating wellness into its portfolio, the business spread risk, increased footfall and tapped into an increasing demographic that was travelling and spending: the wellness-conscious traveller.

Each of these stories lays out the framework of how innovative and forward-thinking hoteliers are using wellness to pivot their businesses to thrive, instead of merely surviving and waiting for things to return to how they were before. My hope is that these examples inspire and challenge you to do the same for your hotel.

CASE STUDY
WELLNESS AS A TOOL TO CREATE SUCCESS STORIES

In this case study, we examine how Ana Beatriz, a hospitality consultant, created a unique, wellness-oriented resort to deliver increased value to both investors and guests. The property is a 70-key resort in Portugal with one food and beverage outlet, complete with a bar, tranquil surroundings, fitness facility and spa.

The challenge

Ana often faces investor pushback due to the misconceptions around wellness in hospitality in the Portuguese market. Hotels centre their wellness concepts around the spa alone, while guests are unaware of the benefits of other wellness experiences.

In this property, the challenge was two-fold:

1. Getting investor buy-in on making wellness an integral part of the hotel offering's DNA when other hospitality consultants were pitching concepts that were more traditional and familiar.

2. Finding the right people who understood wellness to successfully implement and execute the wellness concept. It was a small hotel with a limited budget.

The approach

The investors already had a rudimentary understanding of wellness, which Ana needed to nurture through a compelling proof of concept and a foolproof implementation plan. She developed an offering that went beyond the reputation of traditional wellness as an esoteric practice by delivering high-quality, tangible services that addressed guests' actual wellness needs. Once the concept sketch was approved, she conducted extensive research online and in their network, gathering data on how viable the concept would be in the real world.

With the strong, research-based concept in place, she was then able to gain the buy-in of investors. During the pitch, she demonstrated the rationale for investing in wellness using compelling facts and evidence. Ana's passion for wellness was impactful with the investors and opened them up to the possibilities of increasing the hotel's revenue and adding value through wellness.

She calculated the investment required, and the projected return, by creating investment maps with key information on how wellness was performing globally and in Portugal. These maps helped to manage expectations and give a realistic projection of how the wellness asset would impact the overall value of the hotel.

To demonstrate the tangible value of wellness, she outlined measurable metrics, such as increased ADR, occupancy and average spend. Demonstrating the intangible value of wellness was more challenging; these returns gained are not so easily quantifiable. For instance, market appraisal and guest satisfaction cannot be shown in numbers on paper. To demonstrate these intangible returns, Ana used examples of similar brands, some with wellness offerings and others without. In comparing the two types of hotels, they found that people held hotels with a comprehensive wellness offering in higher regard than those that did not have one.

With the green light from investors, she finally moved to implementation. As the hotel was relatively small and had a limited budget, the wellness facilities and services had to be simple yet functional. The team realised that to differentiate the hotel, they would need to create their special way of doing wellness that was different from other hotels in the region. They wanted to increase their guests' awareness of the role that wellness had on their overall experiences in the hotel. Although there was a clear demographic that demanded wellness services, there was another segment that still needed to be educated. She designed their system so as to cater to the guests' wellness needs from before they arrived at the resort to well after they left.

With the right system in place, the hotel was better positioned to find the people who would execute the wellness concept. The staff consisted of people who believed in wellness themselves and were cognisant of its integral role in the overall hotel offering. Ana opted for a lean and affordable team with the right attitude and trained them to deliver quality wellness experiences, instead of choosing a highly skilled and experienced team that the hotel could not afford.

The outcome

The hotel's wellness asset helped it to stay resilient during the economic hardship brought by the 2020 pandemic. Where other hotels in the region needed to shut down because of low volumes, the resort was recording around 60% occupancy rates. It saw an increase in profitability as more people booked their stay directly with the hotel. The ADR remained stable; people were comfortable paying the price because they understood the value they would be getting in return. The resort also enjoyed an overall improvement in market perception and became the go-to destination for authentic Portuguese wellbeing experiences.

ESSENCE application

The major pain point for any hospitality consultant is shifting the perspective of investors from looking at wellness as a separate part of operations to viewing it as part of their hotel's identity. This resort was successful because of Ana's insistence on making wellness part of the resort's DNA (remember the buster of Myth 3 in Chapter 2?). By putting the wellbeing of the guests at the front and centre of the offering, the resort successfully guided its guests through their journey to live authentic wellbeing experiences, providing them with memorable experiences they could share with their networks.

Endorsement

'I love that Sonal's ESSENCE methodology emphasises the hotel's mission to give holistic wellness to its guests and shows them how to. Without wellness at the centre of the hotel's identity and culture, there can be no comprehensive hospitality.'

- ANA BEATRIZ

CASE STUDY

WELLNESS AS A TOOL TO STAND OUT FROM THE CROWD

This case study examines how Fernando Gibaja, a seasoned general manager in the luxury segment, has used wellness to create a distinctive offering that sets his urban hotel apart from the rest in the Singaporean market. The property is a multi-purpose urban complex with residential keys and a 100-room hotel with a spa, fitness facility and food and beverage outlet.

The challenge

Wellness offerings in Singapore are largely centred on generic spa treatments. Market awareness was low when Fernando first thought to pivot his hotel into wellness.

The challenge he faced was two-fold:

1. Shift in demographics. The pandemic brought a new segment of guests (not his ideal) who were not consciously seeking out wellness experiences; hence Fernando ran the major risk of creating a wellness asset that would be under-appreciated.

2. Market uncertainty and disruption. His ideal guest was actively looking for wellbeing-oriented services, but due to market uncertainty, he had to put wellness at the core with minimal investment to gain owner buy-in and protect cashflow.

The approach

Instead of trying to carry out extensive market research in a place where wellness had no track record, Fernando took the position of a wellness pioneer, opting to innovate and update a wellness concept as the market began to respond. For the concept to succeed in his hotel, he needed to shift the mindset of his owners, staff and guests towards wellness. His first call was to evaluate his options in the current market conditions.

The hotel's demographics had shifted from middle-aged guests before the 2020 pandemic to a slightly younger generation, resulting in a change in guest expectations. The millennials were more tech-savvy and wanted their experiences to be shareable via social media. They also expected quick delivery and a tangible return on their investment; for example, they expected the hotel to recognise special occasions, like birthdays and anniversaries, with a gift of a bottle of champagne or some flowers. In contrast, the slightly older generation sought quality experiences which they were willing to pay for. They wanted a more peaceful stay and to experience the property itself and interact with other guests.

These observations helped Fernando to craft a strong concept that implicitly put the wellness needs of the guest at the forefront of their experience. Fernando devised a clever strategy that tweaked existing services so they would reflect the changing times while simultaneously sticking to the hotel's identity. He opted to invest small sums in fine-tuning services, thereby protecting his owners from substantial initial investments; he was aware that wellness has a long incubation period and returns would take time.

With the stakeholders on board, Fernando's next move focused on getting staff buy-in. All staff had to be retrained on what the hotel wanted to achieve with this new approach. They would play an integral part in raising awareness of the hotel's wellness concept, thus the training – which was rolled out to every hotel employee – focused on creating educational guest interactions.

Fernando laid a solid foundation for the overall concept with his diligent planning. In the rooms, the hotel added wellness accessories like yoga mats for guests to use at their convenience. Dining menus consisted of healthy food and provisions so that detox plans were available any time a guest requested one. Although they kept the traditional treatments in the spa facilities, they updated the treatment menu to appeal to their new client demographic. Every part of the hotel had wellness activities that guests could partake in, such as calligraphy, meditation on the lawn and boba tea classes. These activities were adjusted to accommodate children whenever the need arose, thus avoiding the seasonality of a dedicated kids' club.

To spread the word about their new offering, the hotel partnered with and hosted influencers who had a vibrant following on social media comprised of their ideal audience. This proved to be a more effective marketing strategy than paying a traditional magazine for the same type of exposure.

The outcome

Although the return on investment was expected to kick in after several years, the hotel's wellness asset performed well in the incubation stage. They experienced a spike in long-stay guests from 55% to about 70% of their intake and doubled their projected budget. They also built a more committed and loyal customer base through guests who actively engaged with the brand. More guests shared their experiences at the hotel, thus increasing the hotel's social following and outreach, further strengthening their market position. The success of this initial phase allowed Fernando to get his owners to invest more towards putting wellness at the core of the business.

ESSENCE application

When you take time to carefully plan out your wellness concept, the subtlest of tweaks can change your hotel's trajectory. For Fernando, the concept worked because he believed in wellness himself (remember Harsh Truth 1 from Chapter 4?), saw the opportunity for growth and crafted a strategy that his owners would sign off on without much reservation. Above all, simple yet strategic tweaks helped them stay the course even when the results weren't visible. Fernando's strategy mirrors the ESSENCE methodology by meticulously planning and stepping into the guide role to make the hotel a distinctive destination in Singapore that attracts premium guests in the region and internationally.

Endorsement

'Creating a strong wellness concept takes a lot of time and preparation and you have to be patient. It's like losing weight– if you lose it too quickly, it will come back on, but if you do it slowly, you will consolidate your body and your metabolism will change. The ESSENCE methodology is

strategic in that way, and it helps GMs to make thorough preparations and get the right people on board to create something truly unique.'

– FERNANDO GIBAJA

CASE STUDY

WELLNESS AS A TOOL TO CARVE OUT YOUR OWN NICHE

In this case study, we examine how a family-owned and operated hotel located in the heart of Mumbai is using wellness to create authentic experiences steeped in the local culture. The property is a 20-key boutique hotel with a single treatment room and a multi-purpose communal area used as the lobby, dining area and business centre. The co-founder, Abedin Sham, is both operator and owner of the hotel.

The challenge

The pandemic suddenly cut the hotel's main source of business. The restrictions on international travel forced it to concentrate on the local market – a completely different demographic to its pre-pandemic ideal guest.

The challenge Abedin faced was two-fold:

1. Pivoting his business while maintaining its boutique positioning. He didn't want to introduce temporary measures that would help the hotel survive in the short term but jeopardise its long-term success.

2. Getting co-owner buy-in to do something different. He was aware that the return on investment of adding wellness to his offering would take time and that perhaps the results wouldn't be evident in the beginning.

The approach

Abedin had been studying the market for a while, interviewing other hotel general managers to find out what they were doing. He found that traditional hotels were not adequately providing authentic offerings that allowed guests to experience the city just as a local would– and vice versa, allowing locals to enjoy staycations in their own city. Most of the options available to guests left them feeling like there was still more to do in the city. The traditional hotels concentrated more on the design of the property and focused on selling rooms instead of providing a memorable, holistic experience.

He also observed market behaviours over a period of five years and discovered an under-served market he could tap into. There were people within the city who wanted to escape their regular lives without spending too much money on exotic destinations.

As one of the co-owners of the hotel, Abedin had to spearhead the pivot and ensure that other stakeholders understood his vision. He knew that wellness was perceived as a trend in his market, and he was mindful of not falling into the same trap. He developed a concept that focused on the guest experience. Every part of the guest's wellbeing needs was considered, from nutrition to mental wellness. The concept itself was designed to reflect a strong corporate social responsibility that would help guests engage further with the city.

Abedin invested in a system that displayed the hotel's holistic wellness philosophy. They spent thousands of dollars on a filtration plant that would use reverse osmosis to provide fresh, clean water for the guests to drink using copper jugs. They poured resources into a recycling system, becoming the first hotel in the area to recycle their soap. They removed single-use plastics wherever possible. This environmentally friendly approach attracted guests who shared the same philosophy, and the budget included thank you gifts for almost every guest to show appreciation for their support.

Their concept transcended the traditional hotel wellness offering that was not yielding results for surrounding hotels. They designed their services to give guests a genuine, local experience throughout their stay.

They used the communal space for activities such as sound meditation and yoga classes and transformed it back into the dining room afterwards. The rooms were more spacious than those found in most Mumbai houses; local guests could thus take a breather from their families and have more space to work and socialise without travelling too far from home. This was the perfect alternative for young remote-working professionals who did not have a conducive environment for productivity in their own homes.

In all this, the hotel kept its prices constant, even after the pandemic hit. They risked losing money in the short term; however, they were also assured of attracting the right demographic. The price also protected the essence of the hotel by reflecting the true value of the overall offering.

The outcome

The return on investment came by quicker than Abedin expected; 14 months into the pivot, he had recouped 100% of the principal investment. Instead of the projected five years of incubation, the wellness asset proved successful in just over a year.

In that short space of time, the hotel also enjoyed an increase in guest satisfaction. Many of their guests gave them hand-written notes detailing how profound their experience was – and shared their memorable moments with their networks. Such market reappraisal so early on in the process has positioned the hotel well for future success during the pandemic and well after it has ceased.

ESSENCE application

Abedin's case demonstrates how staying true to the essence of your hotel can yield massive returns. By studying the market and learning what people truly wanted, he identified an opportunity to set his hotel apart from the rest. The hotel's location was not suited for elaborate spas and fitness facilities, hence it used subtle wellness services that fit into the local guests' way of life (remember how we talked about location relevance in Expectation?). Abedin sought to make the local market a stakeholder in the hotel's offering, and his effort paid off well. Basically, he followed the seven ESSENCE principles.

Endorsement

'*A lot of the new offerings from hotels will be vanilla concepts that don't cater to what the clients really want. Sonal's ESSENCE methodology has it right – if you've got the core values right, your wellness asset will succeed.*'

– ABEDIN SHAM

CASE STUDY

WELLNESS AS A TOOL FOR BOOSTING FOOTFALL

This final case study looks at Yagna Prathap's use of wellness to consolidate his company's diverse portfolio of hotels and increase their overall valuation. The property is a four-star, new-build hotel with 800 rooms, 10 food and beverage outlets, three swimming pools, a kids' water park, an entertainment centre and boutique wellness facilities.

The challenge

Before the pandemic, people were already looking for affordable, restorative experiences in the form of staycations and quick, convenient wellness programmes. Post-pandemic, wellness has become the primary concern for most guests.

The challenge Yagna faced was two-fold:

Adapt to new market demand and conditions. The hotel was designed with a different segment and reality in mind.

It now had to adapt to the new market, adhere to pandemic regulations and still make a sustainable income.

Incorporate wellness as an integral part of the offering rather than an amenity. A seven-year return on investment was not a feasible option for them. They needed an effective wellness concept that would yield results in half the normal time and still deliver quality wellness experiences.

The approach

Yagna began the pivot with extensive market research and observing consumer behaviour in his market and hotels. He found that the market no longer sought expensive, grand wellness offerings. Instead, guests wanted affordable luxury they could enjoy without breaking the bank. Thus, long rituals were out of the question as guests preferred quick, convenient treatments so they could get on with their day. Using this information, Yagna was then able to craft a comprehensive offering for this four-star beach hotel.

After careful consideration, he realised their best bet was a compact offering that had all the wellness facilities in one area of the hotel, making operations efficient for the hotel and the facilities convenient for the guests.

At first, the investment company and the operator were not on the same page about the size of the facility. The operator was concerned that the facility would be too small for such a large hotel. On the other hand, the investors did not want to commit to a large concept that had no historical data to prove its viability. This disagreement was fuelled by two major risks that came with creating a small facility.

The first risk was that the demand would far outweigh the supply, and the overall guest experience would be compromised as a result. In a hotel that could accommodate 1,200 guests within its 800 rooms, a wellness facility with only four treatment rooms seemed too small to bear the demand. The operators feared they would have to deal with numerous guest complaints.

The second risk was that the concept itself would not be received well and the facilities' failure would sink the entire hotel. From the investors' viewpoint, adding more facilities would be easier once they had proof that their concept was viable and money was already coming in.

Eventually, both parties agreed on an optimal size for the facility and a relatively small budget. The entire wellness offering covered an area of roughly 1,800 square feet and included a separate entrance for external visitors who wanted quick treatments.

Since the hotel was a four-star resort in a prime location, the team did not put in any costly luxury tiers. Instead, they aptly responded to the guests' expectations with inexpensive wellness facilities that offered quality treatments in one hour or less. This type of affordable luxury attracted locals who had previously been excluded by the cost of more expensive wellness offerings.

Guests would pay a fixed price that covered all their activities; only the wellness treatments were charged separately. The operator remained compliant with regulations, using a booking system that the guests found efficient.

The outcome

Overall, the concept was well received and the hotel has thrived. It has happy guests who enjoy enhanced experiences at just the right price point and has already built a committed, loyal and engaged customer base which has given it a competitive edge in the market.

The hotel's overall footfall increased. Despite the pandemic slowing businesses down, their wellness facilities were booked from 9am to 10pm. Starting small has allowed them to carry out their proof of concept with minimal financial risk. The hotel is now able to reinvest the revenue generated by its wellness offering into bigger facilities after the initial return on investment.

ESSENCE application

The ESSENCE methodology emphasises putting wellness at the centre of operations in the hotel. Yagna did this literally with a centralised and compact design for the hotel's wellness facilities. A long-standing myth in hospitality is that wellness represents a small part of the hotel's profit and loss; in reality, guests expect wellness features to be included in the overall hotel experience. Wellness serves as both a tangible and intangible asset for the hotel (remember Harsh Truth 2 from Chapter 4?). Yagna's apt response to new guest expectations propelled the hotel towards a successful pivot into wellness. In fact, it was the smart approach to start with a small, winning concept so they could reinvest in creating a wellness asset that would future-proof the business.

Endorsement

'We are entering into a very precarious time in our industry where hotels will fight over the same clients, as the demand is limited. The ESSENCE methodology created by Sonal is perhaps the most viable alternative that can help hoteliers adapt and pivot into new territory without breaking budget. If it is done right, this could be the best bet to future-proof the industry.'

– YAGNA PRATHAP

CHAPTER 14
NEXT STEPS

EXPLORING THE INTERSECTION BETWEEN TOURISM AND WELLNESS

Wellness is here and it is here to stay. One of the key takeaways of the 2020 pandemic was the importance of being well and healthy. It didn't matter if our businesses were sent to an incredulous screeching halt overnight. It didn't matter that a few months into the pandemic we knew that this time things were different – the path to recovery for the hospitality and wellness industries would be long. What mattered was that our people – our guests, teams and communities – were safe and healthy. What mattered was being true to our core – our people – and finding a way in which those who had to stay home could be extended the necessary support to get them and their families through the storm. What mattered was our resilience, perseverance and grit to keep afloat. Ultimately, what mattered was our wellbeing.

Innovative and forward-thinking hoteliers put wellness at the core of their business to create properties that are landmarks within their communities, be they urban or resorts. They don't sell room nights, a delicious meal in their Michelin-star restaurant or a heavenly signature massage. Instead, they solve the wellbeing problems of their guests and transform their overall wellbeing, even if that is in small, simple ways.

Innovative and forward-thinking hoteliers understand that, just as each hotel is unique, so is its wellness offering. They take time to get to know their avatars and truly understand their wellbeing problems, and they design their wellness offerings accordingly. They make their guests the hero of their story.

Innovative and forward-thinking hoteliers are astute and unconventional in their approach. They look beyond the physical realms of their hotel and find ways to break away from hospitality's traditional bricks-and-mortar business model. Through wellness, they explore alternative streams of revenue to increase their top and bottom lines. They prolong their guests' journey from before they arrive at the hotel until long after they leave.

Innovative and forward-thinking hoteliers know that what differentiates their offering from that of other hotels is their special way of doing wellness, not the latest shiny equipment or so-called life-changing therapy. They look for smart, simple and effective ways of solving their guests' problems instead of creating grand wellness facilities.

Innovative and forward-thinking hoteliers are empathetic and put their staff's wellbeing front and centre. They focus on making their teams' lives easier and create processes to ensure their staff succeed. As a result, they attract passionate, committed and loyal people who are hoteliers at heart; people who want to make a meaningful impact and make their guests' stay truly special.

Innovative and forward-thinking hoteliers are confident, focused and growth driven. They strategically steer their operations back on track and don't get easily swayed by the latest trends. They are confident with their offering and teams, and persist to constantly improve their guests' landmark experiences.

Innovative and forward-thinking hoteliers have guests who are happy and who leave rave reviews. Their guests live truly unique, special and memorable moments that they want to repeat again and again, and want to share with their networks. As a result, these hotels save money in marketing and advertising spend.

Innovative and forward-thinking hoteliers are visionary and audacious. They create landmark hotels out of the properties they work in. They are sought out by investors, owners and hotel companies because they create profitable, resilient and adaptable businesses. They break away from the traditional mould and make wellness a way of life.

My challenge to you when you put this book down is to be part of this special group of hoteliers who are creating landmark properties and shaping the future of the industry.

I believe there is incredible power at the intersection of tourism and wellness. Humans have travelled for millennia to heal and regenerate themselves and to explore new territories. Hotels are a great place to facilitate this exploration and for people to disconnect, reconnect and live meaningful experiences.

There is no doubt that wellness is a very lucrative business, and I believe there has never been a better moment than now to be in the industry and to make a meaningful impact. Embrace wellness and be part of positively shaping our industry. Leave your own landmarks along the journey.

ARE YOU READY TO PUT WELLNESS AT THE CORE OF YOUR BUSINESS?

Are you ready to put into practice what you have learned in this book? Here are three ways you can tap into the true potential of wellness.

1. Get your ESSENCE score and attend a free Wellness Business Strategy session

Now that you have been through my ESSENCE process, take my scorecard a second time so you can see how much progress you've made and what your new 'snapshot' looks like. You'll get another detailed report on the seven key stages with additional action steps. This will allow you to confidently continue to focus your resources on the right things going forward so you can make the right decisions about creating a profitable, sustainable wellness asset.

I really want you to make a success of this, and I know it can be a big shift in your business. Sign up for one of my Wellness Business Strategy sessions specially designed for hoteliers, where we discuss how you can optimise your wellness offering and the strategic steps you can take to improve profitability in the post-pandemic world.

Take the ESSENCE scorecard here:
www.spa-balance.com/essence-scorecard

2. Join the community

I run the *Wellness in Hospitality* podcast, in which I interview hoteliers from all around the world to understand their insights into the role of wellness in the hospitality industry.

We discuss how each hotelier is managing the situation in a unique way according to the realities of their property.

Subscribe to my *Wellness in Hospitality* podcast here: **www.spa-balance.com/wellness-in-hospitality-podcast**

3. Connect with me

I mainly hang out on LinkedIn, where I share my thoughts and engage with my network about all things related to wellness in hospitality. We have great discussions on a diverse range of topics. Connect with me and join the conversation. I'd love to hear from you.

Say hello to me here: **www.linkedin.com/in/sonaluberoi/.**

GLOSSARY

Avatar: A demographic or target audience that represents the ideal guest you would like to attract to your hotel.

Course correction: When you go off track from your wellness concept and you need to nudge your operations back on track.

Future-proof: To design your hotel's offering so that it continues to be relevant and deliver value well into the future, constantly evolving and responding to changing market conditions.

Guide: A knowledgeable figure with authority, who people trust to guide them through their journey.

Gyroscope: In the context of this book, a type of compass whose orientation is not affected by the tilts of the business landscape (e.g., shifts in market conditions, crises). In the case of your hotel, your gyroscope is your wellness asset, which provides your hotel stability and maintains a reference direction to ensure your business is on track.

Hero: The main character of a story or plot who is on a mission to get to an end destination. The whole plot or scene is set up around them.

Landmark: An event or discovery marking an important stage or turning point in something.

Landmark experiences: Experiences that are authentic, meaningful and memorable to our guests; experiences that make them feel special.

Pitfall: A hidden or unsuspected danger or difficulty.

Playbook: A business playbook contains all the pieces and parts that make up your company's go-to approach for getting things done.

Pre-empt: To take action in order to prevent (an anticipated event) happening.

Service blunder: A careless mistake in service that is not related to lack of skill or expertise, but to clumsiness and lack of attention.

Villain: The bad guy of a story or plot who tries to spoil the plot and scene so that the hero can't get to their end destination.

ACKNOWLEDGEMENTS

My beautiful mother for her unconditional love and for being a source of constant inspiration through her sheer strength, determination and drive. My father for guiding me from up above, having given me the opportunity to enter into one of the most beautiful worlds there is. My inspiring twin brother, Maneesh, and lovely siblings, Ameet and Priya. David, for putting up with my obsession to get this book written.

Stephanie Taylor, for her guidance and support throughout the process. I wouldn't have achieved all I have this year if it weren't for you!

Leila Green, for the hand-holding, patience and motivation at each step of the way, and for bringing clarity, simplicity and structure to complex points. The book certainly would not look the way it does today without you. I'm deeply grateful.

My remarkable beta readers: Gwendolyn Alston, Riaan Drever, Eleonore Astier-Petin, Jerome Hopkins, Tapiwanashe Manhombo and Vanessa Fabiano. Your feedback was priceless. Thank you so much!

Fernando Gibaja, Ana Beatriz, Yagna Prathap and Abedin Sham, for your generosity in sharing your success stories and for believing in wellness.

To the 60+ hoteliers worldwide that I interviewed as part of my research. Thank you for keeping the industry together and inspiring other hoteliers around the world. I hope the industry will find your insights as useful and helpful as I did.

Lightning Source UK Ltd.
Milton Keynes UK
UKHW011959110722
405697UK00002B/327

9 781913 717469